"A nation can survive its fools, and even the ambitious. But it cannot survive treason from within"

The wisdom of Cicero rings as true today as it did when the famed orator addressed the Roman Senate in 50 BCE. Treason is a uniquely dangerous enemy, one masked by a friendly smile that hides its true intentions. It has condemned many rulers to their doom and changed the fate of countries and entire empires. But what does it really mean to be a traitor?

It's time to step into the shadows and meet some of the worst back-stabbers in history. From the notorious Judas Iscariot to Guy Fawkes, Benedict Arnold and the Chinese warrior who murdered his own mentor, prepare to gaze into the dark hearts of the men and women whose names will forever be synonymous with a crime that has inspired countless classic tales and even a hit TV show.

Contents

- 6   Off with their heads!
- 8   All in good faith
- 10   Sealed with a kiss
- 14   The Gunpowder Plot
- 24   And you, Brutus?

- 28   Axis Sally
- 34   The samurai who switched sides
- 36   Once, twice, three times a traitor
- 38   Denmark's greatest traitor
- 44   Athelred's hired muscle
- 46   Seller of state secrets
- 48   Benedict Arnold: America's fallen patriot

CONTENTS

- 52 Pétain: Verdun hero or Vichy traitor?
- 60 Ten tragic days
- 64 The betrayal of Rome
- 68 Mata Hari: Spy or scapegoat?
- 74 Puppet of the Rising Sun
- 76 The Cambridge spy ring
- 80 Ephialtes of Trachis
- 82 Akechi Mitsuhide
- 84 Love thy brother
- 88 Talleyrand
- 94 The infamous Lord Haw-Haw
- 96 Strongman of Burkina Faso
- 98 Sir Roger Casement
- 100 Alcibiades: There and back again
- 106 Selling out the hangman's hit squad
- 108 Vidkun Quisling
- 112 The royal lovers' conquest
- 118 American scoundrel: General James Wilkinson
- 120 Julius and Ethel
- 122 The betrayals of Lü Bu
- 126 Catching America's most damaging spy

OFF WITH THEIR HEADS!

Considered among the worst crimes one can commit, the definition and punishment for treason has changed dramatically over time

WORDS | BEE GINGER

Throughout history there have been countless examples of treachery and treason. From the biblical tale of Judas Iscariot to modern-day reality television villains, we remain fascinated by individuals capable of betraying others for their own sinister ends. But what does it really mean to be a traitor?

The origin of the term traitor comes from the Latin word *tradere*, which means 'to hand over, deliver, or betray', and the word was first recorded as a noun around 1225 in Middle English. Under English law, treason has always been considered the most heinous crime. The most well-known example is probably Guy Fawkes' infamous Gunpowder Plot, a scheme that directly threatened the life of the monarch, King James VI of Scotland and I of England. Had it been successful, the ramifications for both crown and country would have been devastating. However, plotting the death of the monarch is not the only way that treason can be committed.

According to the terms of the Treason Act of 1351 (which came about due to efforts by Parliament to reduce the king's ability to denounce anyone as a traitor by narrowing its definition in law) a number of crimes of varying severity once came under the umbrella of treason, from producing counterfeit money or murdering a royal official to the slightly less provable misdemeanour of failing to provide a male heir to continue the royal line of succession. Giving aid or assistance to any enemies of the state or levying any forms of war against the crown was also classed as treason of the highest order, as was any violation of the queen consort, the king's eldest unmarried daughter, or the wife of the heir to the throne. The Treason Act has subsequently been revised over the years, the legal meaning adjusted numerous times to assuage the fears of those in power.

The only punishment that could be handed down for treason was the death penalty, which came in a number of gruesome forms. The majority of executions were public, unless the condemned was of royal descent, in which case they would be spared hanging and instead beheaded, a method deemed more appropriate for the nobility.

Commoners were not so fortunate. While many women were usually burned at the stake (a horrendous execution that was later abolished due to the smell), men found guilty of treason were hanged, drawn and quartered. This truly barbaric form of execution became statutory in 1352 during the rule of King Edward III and saw the convicted traitor fastened to a wooden hurdle and drawn behind a horse to his place of hanging. Before being fully hanged he would be emasculated and disembowelled then beheaded and quartered. Often the dissected body parts would be put on public display to serve as a warning to the masses in an age where there were no police to enforce the king's laws. This brutal death was thought to discourage would-be traitors.

A serious capital crime such as treason could also evoke an attainder. In English criminal law this was seen as a metaphorical corruption of blood, a stain on the family name, and those in the family would be unable to continue as heirs. The condemned would lose all titles, property and their lives. The first bill of attainder was used in 1321, when Hugh le Despenser, 1st Earl of Winchester, was deemed to be 'attainted' for his support of King Edward II's attempts to prevent his overthrow. Le Despenser, along with his son, Hugh Despenser the Younger, was hanged, drawn and quartered, and his remains were thrown to a pack of dogs.

A similar fate was originally bestowed upon Simon Fraser, 11th Lord Lovat, in 1747. Twice found guilty of treason for his role in the Jacobite Uprisings, he was sentenced to be hanged, drawn and quartered, but a merciful King George II commuted this to beheading. Lovat's execution (the last beheading in Britain) was watched by thousands on Tower Hill in London, and it proved to be quite the show. When a nearby wooden stand collapsed, killing a number of onlookers, Lovat is said to have laughed uproariously even as the blade fell, giving rise to the common phrase 'laughing one's head off'.

The final execution in Britain for treason was the 1946 hanging of Lord Haw-Haw, and in 1998 the punishment for this crime was changed to life imprisonment by the passing of the Crime and Disorder Act.

ABOVE It was common for thousands of people to attend an execution, as this illustration of the beheading of John Dudley, Duke of Northumberland, in 1553 shows

ALL IN GOOD FAITH

Inspired by a bloody 17th-century mutiny off the coast of Australia, *The Traitors* continues to captivate audiences with its Machiavellian contestants

| WORDS | BEE GINGER |

Treason and treachery are not synonymous, as many will have witnessed in the popular television series *The Traitors*. For the uninitiated, *The Traitors* is a psychological competition set in Ardross Castle in the Scottish Highlands and has similarities to the popular board games *Wink Murder* and *Mafia* (the show has inspired its own board game of the same name in both the UK and the United States). The show is based on the popular Dutch series *De Verraders* by Marc Pos and Jasper Hoogendoorn, and in addition to the original Dutch version, the show is now also filmed in several other countries including Sweden, Canada, New Zealand, Australia and the U.S.

The game commences with a team of 22 hopeful contestants all presided over by a host. The premise of the show is to take part in a series of missions and challenges as a team in order to increase the prize money as much as possible for the collective pot (£120,000 in the UK). The catch, however, is that within the group are unknown 'Traitors' plotting together to sabotage the group's efforts in order to pick off the 'Faithful' team members one by one. The Traitors will come together most evenings to decide which faithful contestant they want to "murder" (eliminate). That person will be notified and have to leave the contest immediately without saying goodbye. The other contestants will learn of their departure the following morning over breakfast at the castle. At the end of a day of challenges all players will congregate around the Round Table and discuss

The betrayal that inspired *The Traitors*

In October 1628, the *Batavia*, a Dutch East Indian Company ship, set sail from the Netherlands for the port of Batavia in Indonesia with 340 people on board, including women and children. Part of a fleet of eight vessels commanded by a merchant named Francisco Pelsaert, it was captained by Ariaen Jacobsz and carrying several chests of silver coin as well as jewellery. Also among the passengers was Pelsaert's deputy, Jeronimus Cornelisz, an apothecary who was fleeing charges of heresy in the Netherlands.

Aware that Jacobsz despised the fleet commander, Cornelisz hatched a plot with the captain to mutiny and seize the ship's silver. They were in the middle of their scheme when the *Batavia* was separated from the rest of the fleet by a storm off the Cape of Good Hope near South Africa, and the situation worsened in June 1629 when it ran aground near Beacon Island off the west coast of Australia, claiming 100 lives.

In need of food and water, Pelsaert and Jacobsz took a longboat to the island, but when they found neither they decided to make for the port of Batavia in search of help. Pelsaert remained completely unaware of the plot against him.

Meanwhile, Cornelisz, determined to execute his dastardly plan, left the stricken ship and swam to Beacon Island, where he immediately set about taking control by dividing the survivors into groups. He tricked 20 soldiers led by Wiebbe Hayes into searching for water on another nearby island and then abandoned them there to die. Then, with the aid of fellow conspirators, he waged a campaign of slaughter that saw 125 of the survivors killed, including women and babies. It seemed like he would succeed in wiping out all opposition and claiming the *Batavia*'s wealth. However, his plan to desert Hayes and his men backfired.

Upon finding water, Hayes' troops regained their strength, and when they returned to Beacon Island to discover the horror of Cornelisz's massacre, they fought back. The final clash between the warring sides was disturbed when Pelsaert returned aboard the *Sardam* having found help. Cornelisz and six of his men were tried and hung. Two others were left on mainland Australia. Of the original 340 passengers, only 122 would ever reach the port of Batavia. Among them was Jacobsz, whose ultimate fate remains unknown.

which player they want to banish from the castle before voting. The person who has received the most votes will then reveal which team they are affiliated with: the Faithful or the Traitors. If the number of Traitors drops to two they can then recruit a Faithful rather than murdering them. But it is up to the Faithful if they decide to switch sides or be murdered and leave the game.

It is an intense game of trust, backstabbing and ultimately detection, with a large dose of meltdowns, tears, spectacular lies and questionable justifications, making it edge-of-the-seat viewing. If the loyal Faithfuls have banished all the Traitors by the end of the show they will split the prize between them. However, if the Traitor(s) still remain in the group then they will walk away with all the money themselves.

What makes the show unique is the diverse range of contestants, all with differing personalities and reasons for participating in the show. As a viewer it is easy to become emotionally invested, particularly when there are

ABOVE Surviving contestants sit around the Round Table during Season 2 of the U.S. version of *The Traitors*

contestants we can relate to. When we encounter a group of individuals on a programme like this our minds will likely make a quick judgement based on a combination of all the faces and their features together. This process is called ensemble perception, and the judgement is said to be made in as little as a quarter of a second. It makes it harder for us to realise the telltale signs of duplicity as we have already judged the group as a whole rather than as individuals. As time passes and we learn more about each participant our thoughts and feelings towards them will likely change.

Participants in the show, although duplicitous, are of course not going to face prosecution, but it does highlight that we as an audience remain entranced by treacherous villains, whether we want them to be uncovered or not. Our viewing pleasure is not that dissimilar to that of a mediaeval crowd congregating to witness a public execution – thankfully minus the gore. It also reinforces that you should remain careful who you trust.

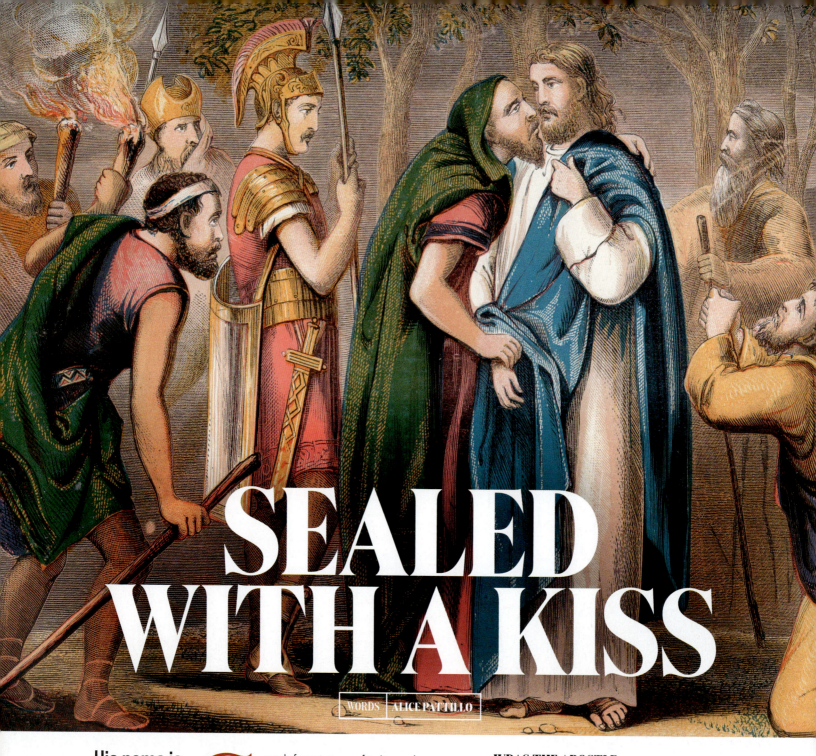

SEALED WITH A KISS

WORDS | ALICE PATTULLO

His name is synonymous with betrayal, but what exactly did Judas do to deserve such an enduring legacy of treachery?

Search for synonyms of traitor and many a reputable thesaurus will offer up the term 'Judas' as a strong substitute for the word. This is all thanks to Judas Iscariot – the most controversial of Jesus' original Twelve Apostles. During the 1st century CE, the name Judas, or the original Hebrew, Judah, was a popular pick for young boys, most commonly associated with a heroic Jewish priest, Judas Maccabeus. But you won't find many Christians brandishing the name since the 2nd century CE – despite its sanctimonious meaning of 'Praise' or 'Let God Be Praised' – as the infamous Judas Iscariot forever tarnished it with his shocking 'betrayal' of Jesus. According to the Biblical Gospel of Matthew, Judas Iscariot – Jesus' seemingly loyal disciple – sold out his good friend to the Romans for 30 pieces of silver, resulting in Christ's crucifixion. But does he deserve his reputation as Christianity's most notorious turncoat, or has history done Judas dirty?

JUDAS THE APOSTLE

There is very little reliable information regarding Judas himself to be found in the Bible. In fact, there is very little reliable information at all. There was no journalistic integrity in the 1st century, and many contemporary accounts, even those presented as fact, include conjecture, propaganda and biased beliefs and opinions. The biblical gospels themselves often contradict one another, telling the same stories from various points of view, and historians have had a notoriously difficult time deciphering whether there is any solid evidence for the majority of its content – including those named within it – and the existence of Judas is largely disputed. However, if indeed he did live, here is what we know about him: Judas was one of Jesus' disciples and the Twelfth of Jesus' Apostles – a member of Jesus' inner circle, if you will – named in all four of Christianity's canonical gospels (that is the synoptic Gospels of Matthew, Mark and Luke and the Gospel of John). Judas is often credited as being the most well-educated of all the Twelve Apostles, brought into the fold

SEALED WITH A KISS

by Nathaniel, largely thanks to his experience with finances, and he became their treasurer – a role that indicates Jesus must have had some trust in Judas. According to the Gospel of Matthew, all of Jesus' apostles were granted the power to cast out demons and heal sickness and disease – or at least were given some early medicinal knowledge and authority in order to perform so-called miracles.

JUDAS THE TRAITOR

Following the Last Supper, Judas went to religious authorities and agreed to take them to Jesus in the Garden of Gethsemane, where he was praying, in return for 30 pieces of silver. He directs the authorities to take whoever he kisses into custody and proceeds to address Christ and kiss him. Jesus responds, according to Matthew, referring to Judas as "friend" but is immediately arrested and turned over to Roman soldiers to be crucified. It is, therefore, essentially Judas' fault that Christ died on the cross.

The canonical scripture concedes that Jesus was aware of Judas' treachery but made no effort to stop him, indicating that it was part of God's plan, and there were no real red flags that Judas would be his downfall; a man like Judas would have had to leave his home and given up his profession in order to follow Jesus around Israel. So, what made Judas change from a seemingly devoted follower and member of Jesus' most elite fraternity to enemy number one?

JUDAS' MOTIVATIONS

There are two main theories as to why Judas betrayed Jesus: greed and Satanic possession. The Gospel of Luke ascertains that Satan entered Judas' body at the time of his betrayal. John also places the blame on demonic influence and one of the seven deadly sins. According to John, Judas was always a bad man and used his role as the group's treasurer to embezzle money and left the Last Supper with the distinct intention of betraying his leader. Curiously, the Gospel of John doesn't mention him trading his loyalty for 30 pieces of silver. The Gospels of Matthew and Mark also blame Judas' greed, but there are a few problems with this theory. Why would Jesus, the most perceptive of all men, choose a greedy and dishonest man to be one of his Twelve? Why wouldn't Judas ask for more than 30 pieces of silver – a small amount to ask for – and why would a man who was driven by greed join up with a penniless group of religious rebels? Some have argued that Judas may have had a political motive and wanted to be named the leader of the Jews, but there is no scriptural evidence for this.

Other theories as to why Judas betrayed Christ abound, including the idea that Judas was angry that Jesus was not the Messiah that the Jews had been promised, or that Judas didn't intend to betray Jesus at all and the idea that he was treacherous is a mistranslation of "hand over", and that he believed they were to speak to Jesus and resolve their differences, therefore explaining why he felt such regret afterwards and, in many instances, is believed to have committed suicide. In any case, Judas had to betray Jesus in order to fulfil the prophecy and for Christ to die as a necessary part of God's salvation plan.

THE DEATH OF JUDAS

According to the Gospel of Matthew, when Judas discovers that his betrayal resulted in Jesus being crucified, he is overcome with guilt. He attempts to return the 30 pieces of silver, which are not accepted due to them being exchanged as blood money. He disregards the silver and commits suicide by hanging. It is unclear why he does this, but various interpretations include sheer horror and regret at

ABOVE *The Last Supper* by Leonardo da Vinci, c. 1495–98

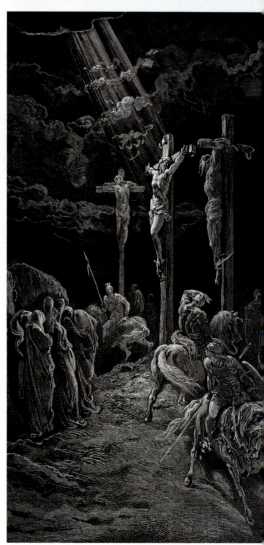

portrays Judas Iscariot as a loyal and devoted disciple of Jesus who only 'sold out' his master by his master's own instruction in order to fulfil God's plan. According to this gospel, Jesus took Judas aside during Passover and revealed secret information to him regarding God and creation (the 'true gospel'), confiding in him that he was the most important of all his disciples and enlisting him to hatch a plan that will result in his own death. Jesus instructs Judas to hand him in to the authorities in order to aid him in releasing his immortal, spiritual self from his mortal, material body. Judas does as Christ asks but later displays penance and anxiety over the act, having a vision of Jesus' other disciples persecuting and stoning him.

THE GOSPEL ACCORDING TO JUDAS

Historically speaking, this gospel gives insight into some of the differences in thought and belief between the various early Christian sects, most notably the Gnostics. Gnosticism is a series of religious ideologies that spread among early Christian groups. The Gnostics were concerned with philosophical questions surrounding existence. Like Christianity, they believed in dualism and a separation between the material body and the immaterial spirit. They had a fundamental belief that the material world is inherently evil, and perhaps even the creator too, while the spiritual world is good and that salvation can only be achieved through spiritual knowledge – which, according to their Gospel of Judas, Judas possessed. However, their focus was not on rituals, enforced behaviours and participation in large institutions like churches; they were more concerned with the self and internalised motivation.

Despite many of their beliefs aligning with Christianity and many gnostics belonging to Christian sects, Gnostic teachings were denounced as heresy by the Church – who didn't like any other interpretations or beliefs being perpetuated that were not their own – and the groups were largely suppressed by the 6th century. However, they survived in esoteric circles and their beliefs endured underground for centuries, later influencing the Renaissance. It is impossible to know who was, and is, right or wrong in terms of the story of Judas – the mainstream church or the gnostic Christian sects – but the Gospel of Judas no doubt throws a spanner in the works when it comes to modern-day mainstream Christian beliefs regarding Jesus' death and Judas' role as a traitor. This missing link, however, seems to give some understanding as to why Jesus refers to Judas as "friend" when he has just betrayed him to Roman authorities, and it also explains away any doubts that Christ could have made a mistake and potentially had a lapse in judgement when selecting his Twelve Apostles.

ETERNAL DAMNATION

Whether Judas was just a poor soul fated to reluctantly sell out his friend, a turncoat non-believer who changed his mind, a victim of the devil's corruption or a manipulative deceiver infected by greed, there is no doubt he remains one of history's greatest traitors – a title he may or may not deserve. His fateful kiss – an act that would usually signify loyalty and love – led to Christ's brutal death, and the term 'Judas kiss' has been immortalised as a phrase used to denote a gesture of friendship that disguises a treacherous deed.

---

the result of his actions (some suggest he thought he was turning Jesus in to the authorities for mere questioning), the fact that he would be cast out by his peers, or in order to seek redemption. Conversely, Acts gives a different story: Judas buys a field with his money and dies by accident, showing no remorse. Others believe he was struck down by the wrath of God.

TRUTH IN THE NAME?

There are conflicting views regarding Judas' second name, Iscariot. One theory is that it is used to differentiate him from other men named Judas found within the gospels and a Greek translation of a Hebrew phrase meaning 'man from Kerioth', a theory supported by the book of John that states that he is "the son of Simon Iscariot". However, other scholars believe that it is an epithet derived from a Latin word, *sicarius*, meaning 'dagger man', associating him with the Sicarii, a group of Jewish rebel assassins. This theory is dubious as there is no other way in which Judas is linked to the gang. Another theory is that the name Iscariot is derived from Hebrew or Aramaic with the meaning of 'false one' or 'liar', but seeing as the gospel writers almost always follow his name with a comment of his betrayal, this also seems a little strange.

JUDAS THE LOYAL FRIEND?

A non-canonical gnostic gospel, the Gospel of Judas, was discovered in the 1970s in Egypt. Found within a codex written upon papyrus in Coptic (an ancient Egyptian language) and bound in leather, the document was carbon-dated to the 2nd or 3rd century CE. The manuscript, which was finally translated in 2006, is said to have been a translation from an earlier Greek text and presents the story of Jesus' crucifixion from Judas' point of view. In contrast to the canonical gospels, the Gospel of Judas

ABOVE Judas remorsefully attempting to return the 30 pieces of silver he received for betraying Jesus

OPPOSITE *The Disembowelment of Judas*, a medieval fresco by Giovanni Canavesio showing the devil devouring his soul

LEFT The result of Judas' treachery – a wood engraving depicting the crucifixion of Jesus Christ by Gustave Doré

> "OTHERS BELIEVE HE WAS STRUCK DOWN BY THE WRATH OF GOD"

THE GUNPOWDER PLOT

Everyone remembers the fifth of November, but the true story of the men who plotted to blow up Parliament is all too often forgotten

WORDS | FRANCES WHITE

When Queen Elizabeth I drew her last breath in 1603, Catholics around England let out their own sighs of relief. Life during her 44-year reign had not been easy. Perhaps in retaliation to the brutal rule of her sister Mary, the devout Catholic queen, Elizabeth had introduced a range of legislations that hit Catholics hard. She was likely fearful of Catholics, and she had reason to be, as a papal bull declared that a Catholic's allegiance was not to the Crown but to God. In one swift move, every Catholic in England was branded a traitor. Simply being a Catholic, or even sheltering Catholics, was not only illegal but akin to high treason. Terrified but devoted to their faith, Catholics were forced underground, and some 130 priests were executed. As the queen aged many of the people who had suffered most under her reign began to hope for a successor who would be more sympathetic to their plight.

Considering how much was at stake, the crown passed to its next bearer incredibly smoothly. James I was the grandson of Henry VIII's sister, Margaret, Queen of Scots, and although he was a Protestant, his mother had been a devout Catholic. For the struggling Catholics, King James's early acts to relax the fines that they suffered were very encouraging. However, this joy quickly turned sour. Realising how the fines filled up the treasury, James reinstalled them and openly damned the Catholic faith. The hopes of many Catholics were crushed, and for some this was the final straw.

If one man had felt the bitter sting of anti-Catholicism in England, it was Robert Catesby. A man from an illustrious family line that stretched back to William Catesby, trusted adviser of Richard III, his entire life he had watched his family's wealth be chipped away by harsh fines. When Catesby was only eight years old he witnessed his father arrested and tried for harbouring a priest. For the remainder of his young years his father was constantly in and out of prison. Catesby was tall, handsome and gifted, but he had been forced to drop out of his studies, as obtaining his degree required him to take the oath of supremacy, which swore allegiance to the queen and the Church of England. The Protestant monarchy had taken everything in Catesby's life: his childhood, his father, his fortune and his future.

Catesby possessed not only good looks but also a generous and affable nature, and as a result he had amassed a large and powerful circle of friends. His allegiance to the Catholic faith was no secret, and he had taken part in a previous rebellion. When Elizabeth fell ill in 1596, Catesby was arrested simply because the government feared he would take advantage of the situation and organise an uprising. Catesby's experiences typified the lives of all Catholics of the time; he was the beating heart of the Catholic struggle, and he was rich and influential enough to actually do something about it.

Catesby had a plan. Killing the king was not enough; Elizabeth's demise had proved that the death of a monarch did not ensure change. The status quo was against him, so the status quo needed to change. To do this, he would blast it to smithereens. In February 1604, Catesby invited Thomas Wintour and John Wright to his house. Wintour, Catesby's cousin, had also felt the sting of anti-Catholicism as his own uncle had been executed for being a priest. Wright was an old friend of Catesby's and had taken part in a rebellion against Elizabeth. In his house in Lambeth, Catesby revealed his grand plan – he would re-establish Catholicism by blowing up the House of Lords during the opening of Parliament. Not only would the king be present but also the most powerful Protestants in the land. The attack would produce a power vacuum, and the long-suffering Catholics would be poised to fill it.

Understandably, Wintour was shocked by his cousin's plans. He was quick to argue that, should they fail, it would put back their cause several years. Catesby responded: "The nature of the disease requires so sharp a remedy." He launched into an impassioned speech about the righteousness of his cause and how Parliament was the perfect target as "in that place they have done us all the mischief". Catesby's natural charisma quickly won around his cousin, who pledged his loyalty and life to the impassioned rebel.

Catesby had recruited his first co-conspirators, and more were to follow. Seeking support from Catholic Spain, Wintour travelled to Flanders. Although he struggled to obtain Spanish support, while there he sought out the man who was fated to become the face of the gunpowder plot – Guy Fawkes. Fawkes had made his Catholic allegiance very clear by fighting on the side of Spain during the Eighty Years' War and had been attempting to drum up support in the country. He was tall, well built with a mop of thick red-brown hair, and he was also determined, driven and skilled in all matters of war. However, there was one of Fawkes' talents that

> "THE STATUS QUO NEEDED TO CHANGE. TO DO THIS, HE WOULD BLAST IT TO SMITHEREENS"

RIGHT Four of the plotters were killed on 30 January, and the other four were executed the following day

BELOW A royal warrant suggested that if 'gentler tortures' proved fruitless, Guy Fawkes should be racked

Catholic crime & punishment

Life for Catholics was anything but easy under the Protestant monarchs

Crime	Punishment
Not attending Anglican service	Initially fined 12 shillings, then raised to £20 per month
Attending a private Catholic mass	Imprisonment
Not paying fines	Imprisonment
Fleeing abroad for longer than six months without permission	Forfeit the profits of lands and all goods
Being a Catholic priest	Death
Refusing to accept the monarch as head of the Church	Imprisonment and death
Reconciling any person to the Catholic Church	Death

THE GUNPOWDER PLOT

Turbulent times

In the years following Henry VIII's break from Rome the religion of the reigning monarch swung from Protestant to Catholic, with devastating effects for their subjects

Henry VIII | Edward VI | Lady Jane Grey | Mary I | Elizabeth I
James VI and I | Cromwell | Charles II | James II | William III

* Charles I, who reigned from 1625–1649, followed the Anglican form of worship but married Henrietta Maria of France, a staunch Catholic, in 1625

The conspirators

Thomas Bates
1567-1606
Role: Catesby's servant
Born in Warwickshire, Bates was employed as Catesby's servant and was seen as a hard-working and loyal man. Due to his close proximity to Catesby he became suspicious of his unusual activity and was invited into the plot. He became a useful accomplice – as an ordinary man he could perform many actions without arousing suspicion.

Robert Wintour
1568-1606
Role: Financial support
The oldest Wintour brother, Robert inherited the majority of his father's estate, including Huddington Court. Through marriage Robert aligned himself to a strong Catholic family, and his home became a refuge for priests.

Christopher Wright
1570-1605
Role: Conspirator
The younger of the Wright brothers, Christopher was described as taller, fatter and fairer than John. A private and discreet man, since his conversion he was fully committed to the Catholic faith and took part in the same rebellion as his brother and Catesby.

John Wright
1568-1605
Role: Original conspirator
The older of the two Wright brothers, John was a school friend of Guy Fawkes and was thrown in prison for taking part in rebellions. With a reputation as a brave, loyal and skilled swordsman, he converted to Catholicism and became associated with Catesby.

THE GUNPOWDER PLOT

Thomas Percy
1560-1605
Role: Logistics
Percy had a reputation as a wild youth, having possibly abandoned his wife and killed a Scotsman in a skirmish. When Percy converted to Catholicism it helped to calm some of his more rebellious ways, funnelling his fiery nature into bettering the Catholic cause in England.

Guy Fawkes
1570-1606
Role: Explosives expert
Born in York, Fawkes lost his father at a young age, and when his mother married a Catholic he converted to the faith. He fought for Spain in the Eighty Years' War and adopted the Italian form of his name, Guido. He was furiously opposed to James I, describing him and all of Scotland as heretics.

Robert Catesby
1573-1605
Role: Leader
The only surviving son of Sir William Catesby, Robert Catesby gained a reputation as a Catholic sympathiser after taking part in a rebellion in the hopes of usurping the queen. Desperate to reclaim Catholic power, Catesby concocted a plot that would require the co-operation of only a few trusted men but was capable of destroying Protestant power in England.

Thomas Wintour **1571-1606**
Role: Original co-conspirator
Thomas Wintour was intelligent, witty and well educated. He fought against Catholic Spain, but his views quickly changed and he became a faithful Catholic. Thomas travelled to Spain in an attempt to drum up support, also known as the Spanish treason, but he was unsuccessful and thereby driven to other, more drastic methods.

attracted Catesby in particular – his proficiency and knowledge of gunpowder.

When the men met again at the Duck and Drake Inn, they had drafted another conspirator, Thomas Percy, a dear friend of Catesby's. Percy had a reputation as a wild and rebellious youth. He had attempted to build a strong relationship with James I for the good of his religion but now felt the bitter sting of betrayal. Percy, on a previous occasion, had to be stopped by Catesby from storming into the palace and taking down the king single-handedly. Together, these five passionate and wronged men met in the Catholic safe house and Catesby outlined the plan. Percy's support was almost a given, and he proclaimed, "Shall we always, gentlemen, talk and never do anything?" Swayed either by their enigmatic leader or their own hatred of Protestants, the five men swore an oath of secrecy upon a bible and received the Holy Communion from a priest secretly celebrating mass, completely unaware that the men were planning regicide.

With his first co-conspirators in place, Catesby sprung into action. The opening of Parliament had been postponed until 5 November the following year due to plague. This gave him plenty of time to prepare everything. Initially, Catesby figured the best way to get the gunpowder beneath the House of Lords would be to dig a tunnel, but the men soon realised a far safer way was to lease one of the storerooms that lay beneath. Luckily, Percy had a business in London, so he could easily lease a storeroom without attracting suspicion. Explosives expert Guy Fawkes posed as John Johnson, Percy's servant, and was placed in the premises. The conspirators stored the gunpowder in Catesby's house and gradually ferried it across the Thames into the dwelling under the cover of darkness.

Steadily, more men were drafted into the conspiracy, as it proved impossible for five men alone to handle such grand plans. Catesby's servant, Bates, became suspicious, and his master had no option but to recruit him. Robert Keyes, Robert Wintour, John Grant and Christopher Wright were also all inducted. Not only were they all passionate Catholics, but many possessed large fortunes and manor houses that would aid the cause.

Secretly, Catesby was worried. He wasn't a terrorist motivated by blind revenge, he was a moral and religious man, and he wanted to be sure that what he was doing was right. Struggling with his conscience, he repeatedly visited two priests, Father Henry Garnet and Oswald Tesimond. Catesby had no doubts that the king was guilty, but he worried about the innocent people who would inevitably be killed in the blast. He asked if this could be excused: was it okay to kill innocents for the greater good? Sworn to the law of confession, Garnet could tell no one of Catesby's plot, but he attempted to dissuade him.

Despite the priests' warnings, Catesby continued bringing gunpowder into the storage hold. He also began

ABOVE Guy Fawkes' signature before torture (top) and after (bottom)

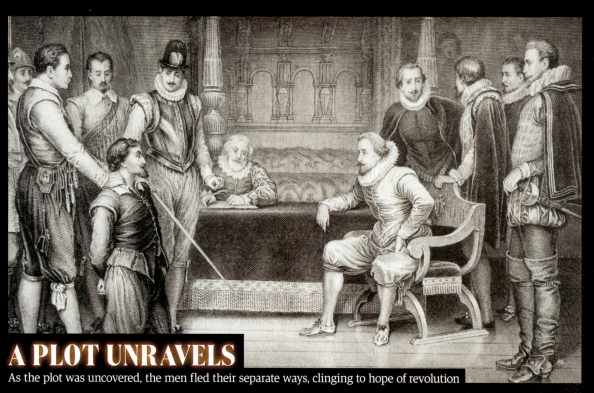

A PLOT UNRAVELS
As the plot was uncovered, the men fled their separate ways, clinging to hope of revolution

Evening 4 November
Westminster
Catesby, John Wright and Bates decide that the plot will go ahead, despite the discovery that a warning letter was sent to Monteagle, and begin setting out towards the Midlands.

Night 4 November
Parliament vaults
The king's men search the vaults under Parliament. They stumble upon Fawkes standing by a pile of wood, who informs them that his name is John Johnson and that he works for Thomas Percy.

Late night 4 November
Parliament vaults
Under the king's orders, the men return to the vault and find Fawkes dressed ready for a getaway. He is immediately arrested and taken to the king in the early hours of 5 November.

Morning 5 November
Westminster
Christopher Wright learns of the plot's discovery and rushes to the Duck and Drake Inn to inform Thomas Wintour. Wintour warns those still in London – Percy, Keyes and Rookwood.

Midday 5 November
Near Milton Keynes
Rookwood rides furiously for two hours and manages to catch up with Catesby and the others to warn them of the plot's failure and Fawkes's arrest. They decide to continue on to Dunchurch.

6 p.m., 5 November
Ashby St Ledgers
The six fleeing conspirators meet up with Robert Wintour, then continue on and meet with Digby, who is accompanied by a hunting party. They continue west to Warwick.

THE GUNPOWDER PLOT

to make plans for the second part of their scheme. Eager to maintain some order after the king's death, he decided that James' child, Princess Elizabeth, would be put in place as his successor. At only eight years old he believed she could be moulded into the figurehead they desired. Elizabeth was also located not in London but in Coombe Abbey near Coventry. In order to make sure this final step went off without a hitch, Catesby recruited the last three conspirators: Ambrose Rookwood, Everard Digby and Francis Tresham.

By October, everything was in place. Fawkes would remain in London and light the fuse before escaping the city and travelling to Europe to drum up support. Meanwhile, in the subsequent madness, a revolt would break out in the Midlands and Elizabeth would be captured. Catesby seemed to have recovered from his earlier concern, but the same could not be said of his co-conspirators. A number of the men had friends in Parliament who were fellow Catholics. Late in the evening on 26 October, a letter arrived at the house of one of these fellow Catholics, Lord Monteagle, who had in his youth played a part in Catholic plots himself. The contents of the letter were shocking. It warned him to abstain from attending Parliament on 5 November, as "They shall receive a terrible blow, this Parliament." Taking the threat seriously, Monteagle alerted the Earl of Salisbury.

News of the letter quickly found its way back to Catesby, and Tresham was immediately suspected, as

> "KILLING THE KING WAS A STEP TOO FAR; EVEN HIS FELLOW CATHOLICS DESERTED HIM"

BOTTOM RIGHT After his arrest, Fawkes was imprisoned in the Tower of London

BELOW The men at Holbeach House were stripped of their clothes and possessions before being taken to prison

OPPOSITE James I described Guy Fawkes as possessing "a Roman resolution"

Monteagle was his brother-in-law. Catesby and Thomas Wintour furiously confronted the new recruit, threatening to hang him for his idiocy, but Tresham was able to convince his fiery leader of his innocence. However, Catesby was unwilling to listen to Tresham's urges to abandon the plot – he was too committed. Risks be damned, the plot would go ahead as planned.

Meanwhile, the king had learned of the mysterious letter. Unlike many of his advisers, he took the warning very seriously. However, he decided to bide his time until the night in question and see if the conspirators would carry out their alleged plot. When 4 November dawned, both the king and Catesby leapt into action. Catesby, with John Wright and Bates, left for the Midlands to launch the second part of the plan while Fawkes prepared for his pivotal part.

The king was preparing too. James' men were searching all the buildings around Parliament for signs of anything suspicious. It was in the cellar during one of these searches that they stumbled upon Fawkes. Dressed as a serving man, he stood before a large, suspicious pile of firewood. He explained that he was a servant of Percy though came across rather desperate. Apprehensive but not willing to upset him further, the men left to report their findings to the king. As soon as James heard Percy's name he was suspicious and ordered another search of the cellar. When the men returned Fawkes was still there. Dressed in his hat, cape and spurs ready for a

Morning 6 November
Warwick Castle
Catesby and his men raid the castle for supplies, arming themselves for the fight they believe will follow, before continuing to Norbrook, where they pick up more weapons.

Afternoon 6 November
Huddington
The conspirators arrive in Huddington and meet with Thomas Wintour. Despite Catesby's hopes, nobody is willing to ally with them, and they are forced to continue alone.

Evening 6 November
London
The Lord Chief Justice questions Rookwood's servants and uncovers the identity of several of the men involved, including Catesby, Rookwood and Wintour.

Evening 6 November
Tower of London
With Guy Fawkes' resolve still holding, James permits the use of torture to loosen his tongue. He orders that 'gentler tortures' are used first.

Night 7 November
Tower of London
After enduring the horrors of the rack, Guy Fawkes finally confesses the details of the plot as well as the names of his fellow co-conspirators.

Night 7 November
Holbeach House
The fugitives arrive at Holbeach House. They spread out their damp gunpowder before a fire and many of them are set alight. Some of the men choose to leave.

Morning 8 November
Holbeach House
200 men led by the Sheriff of Worcestershire besiege Holbeach House. In the gunfight, Catesby, Percy and the Wright brothers are killed. The others are arrested.

21

BELOW People lit bonfires as soon as the news of the plot spread to celebrate the king's survival

quick getaway, he was arrested and searched. Although he stuck to his story and insisted his name was John Johnson, they discovered matches and touchwood on his person. The king's men inspected the firewood and uncovered 36 barrels of gunpowder, enough to blow the Houses of Parliament sky high.

Everything now rested with Fawkes. The plot had failed, that much was obvious, but if he held out long enough the lives of his friends could be saved. As Fawkes was questioned he displayed remarkable courage in the face of almost certain death. He stuck by his story that he was indeed John Johnson. However, he did not for a moment deny his intentions, proclaiming that it was his plan to destroy the king and Parliament. When asked for the names of his accomplices he was insistent he acted alone. James was impressed by Fawkes' resilience, but he needed names, and if torture would loosen his tongue, so be it.

News of Fawkes' arrest quickly spread to the other conspirators. The men who remained in London fled. Percy, aware that his name would be linked to the crime, proclaimed, "I am undone!" Rookwood, an exceptional rider, furiously rode in Catesby's direction to warn him. His incredible ride saw him travel 48 kilometres (30 miles) in just two hours. He arrived breathlessly at Catesby's side and informed him of the plot's uncovering. Catesby was crushed. He had poured everything into this revolution and was desperate to cling onto any hope he could find. He proclaimed that he could still gather enough support for an armed uprising. He knew enough resentful Catholics for an insurrection, and one way or another he would have his rebellion.

The plotters could have left. There was enough time for them to flee England with their lives, but their commitment to their passionate leader and their belief in the cause was so great that they remained by his side. The men continued on to the Midlands, but the support Catesby had promised did not come. Word of the treasonous plot had spread rapidly through the country, faster than the men could travel, and even their friends and families turned them away. Catesby had fatally misjudged the situation. Killing the king was a step too far – even his fellow Catholics had deserted him. Wet, miserable and dejected, when the men finally reached their safe house of Holbeach House in Staffordshire, they spread out their gunpowder in front of a fire to dry it off. A spark ignited it and Catesby, Rookwood and Grant were engulfed in flames.

Meanwhile, in London, the king's men were steadily breaking Fawkes' steely resolve. He was placed upside down in manacles and hung from a wall then most likely strapped to the rack, his limbs agonisingly dislocated. By 7 November, what remained of Fawkes' resolve had crumbled. Broken and drained, he confessed the details of the plot and the names of all his co-conspirators.

Catesby was alive, but for some the explosion was a grim sign, and their commitment to their leader finally waned. Gradually, the team began to unravel. Digby headed to the authorities; Bates, Littleton and Robert Wintour also made their escape. Eventually, all who remained were Catesby, Percy, Thomas Wintour, the Wright brothers, a wounded Rookwood, and Grant, who had been blinded by the fire. Defeated and broken, when the 200 armed government men descended on the group

The Gunpowder conspiracy
Was the plot really concocted by the state?

THE MYSTERY Much of the suspicion surrounding the plot has involved, in some part, the role of the Earl of Salisbury. It was Salisbury who Monteagle alerted upon receiving the letter, and his peculiar actions have prompted many to ponder if he had more knowledge of the plot than he let on. First of all, he failed to immediately inform the king of the plot, who was out hunting and did not return for several days. Salisbury's involvement in the plot actually began before the letter even arrived, as he was aware that something was being planned. When the king did learn of the letter Salisbury denied this knowledge completely and allowed the king to take full credit. This may have been a clever political play, but perhaps it hints at more.

THE MOTIVE The foiling of the plot benefited the king immensely. The feeling of goodwill towards the monarch encouraged Parliament to grant astonishingly high subsidies for the king, and the thanks for this lay at Salisbury's feat. An ambitious man, Salisbury expertly exploited the situation to garner favour with the monarch, and it also allowed him to introduce more anti-Catholic legislation. Salisbury's anti-Catholic feelings far outstripped the monarch's, and he wished to rid England of the religion once and for all.

HIS INVOLVEMENT Conspiracy theorists summarise that Salisbury may have invented the entire plot himself, targeting known Catholic agitators and penning the letter to Monteagle. Others argue that instead of inventing it, Salisbury infiltrated the plot far earlier than the letter reveal and simply allowed it to continue, knowing that he could use it later to fuel the fire of anti-Catholicism.

EVIDENCE The ease in which the conspirators conducted the plot is the main evidence here. The fact that they were able to get 36 barrels of gunpowder in a country where gunpowder was strictly controlled by the government and store them under the Houses of Parliament raises suspicions. However, the lack of any other evidence makes this conspiracy impossible to prove. If Salisbury invented the plot, it is unlikely all the men would have confessed to the crime knowing that death would be the result. The more likely conclusion is that Salisbury was a quick thinking opportunist, who, upon uncovering the truth, exploited the situation for all that it was worth.

THE GUNPOWDER PLOT

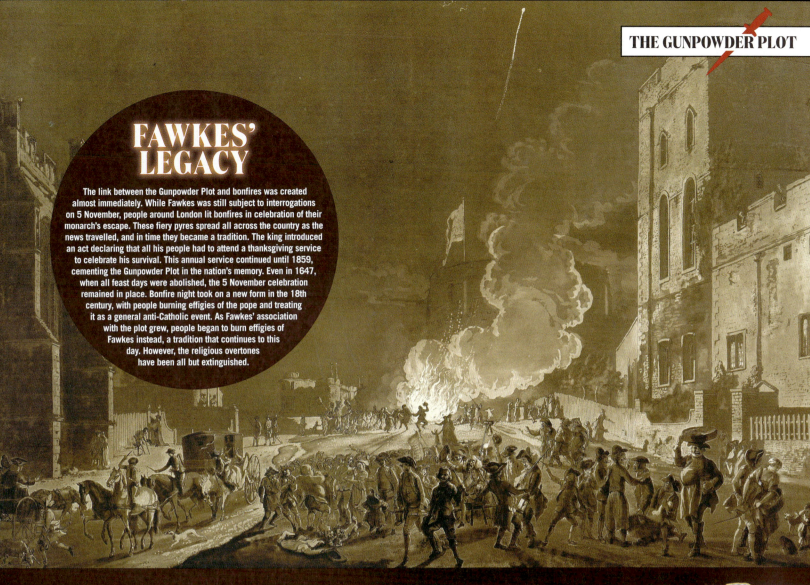

FAWKES' LEGACY

The link between the Gunpowder Plot and bonfires was created almost immediately. While Fawkes was still subject to interrogations on 5 November, people around London lit bonfires in celebration of their monarch's escape. These fiery pyres spread all across the country as the news travelled, and in time they became a tradition. The king introduced an act declaring that all his people had to attend a thanksgiving service to celebrate his survival. This annual service continued until 1859, cementing the Gunpowder Plot in the nation's memory. Even in 1647, when all feast days were abolished, the 5 November celebration remained in place. Bonfire night took on a new form in the 18th century, with people burning effigies of the pope and treating it as a general anti-Catholic event. As Fawkes' association with the plot grew, people began to burn effigies of Fawkes instead, a tradition that continues to this day. However, the religious overtones have been all but extinguished.

on 8 November, the fugitives had no hope of mounting a defence.

The fight was brief. Wintour was shot first followed by the Wright brothers and Rookwood. Catesby and Percy managed to summon the last embers of their fiery zeal and made a final stand together at the door. When they fell it was as one, downed by a single bullet. On the edge of death and bleeding out, Catesby used his final ounce of strength to drag himself to a picture of the Virgin Mary, and cradling it in his arms, breathed his last.

The men who died at the house – Catesby, Percy and the Wright brothers – were lucky. Those who remained were rounded up, arrested and thrown in prison. Under threat of torture all of the men admitted their involvement in the plot. Before the trials even began the verdict was a foregone conclusion. The men were paraded up and jeered at by a furious audience. The conspirators had no defence so could only utter their own pleas for mercy. Rookwood in particular spoke for all the men when he said he was "neither actor nor author" and had acted out of blind devotion to their ringleader, Catesby, "whom he loved above any worldly man".

The people didn't care how charismatic their leader was – they wanted blood, and they were going to get it. The men were declared guilty of treason, and on a chilly 30 January, the first four faced their punishment. They

> "UNDER THREAT OF TORTURE ALL OF THE MEN ADMITTED THEIR INVOLVEMENT IN THE PLOT"

were dragged through the street strapped to a wooden panel on the back of a horse. Then, the men were stripped down to their shirts and their heads placed in a noose. They were briefly hung but cut down while still breathing so they could experience the pain of having their genitals cut off and burned before their eyes. The bowels and the heart were then removed and the bodies cut into pieces and displayed for the birds to pick at. The bodies of Catesby and Percy were also decapitated and their heads exhibited as a grim warning.

Only one man, the final one to face his punishment, managed to escape the pain of emasculation and disembowelling – Guy Fawkes. Broken and barely able to stand, he summoned his final ounce of strength to leap from the gallows and break his neck, dying instantly (Fawkes, Thomas Wintour, Rookwood and Keyes were put to death on 31 January, a day after Digby, Grant, Bates and Robert Wintour).

The plan had been a disastrous failure, and the unearthing of such a dangerous Catholic plot that almost ended in tragedy did little to help the lives of Catholics in England. Although James was quick to make it clear that he did not blame all the Catholics in his nation, strict laws against them were soon implemented. True Catholic emancipation would take a further 200 years, and the men who had schemed, fought and died for it would live on only in legend and rhyme.

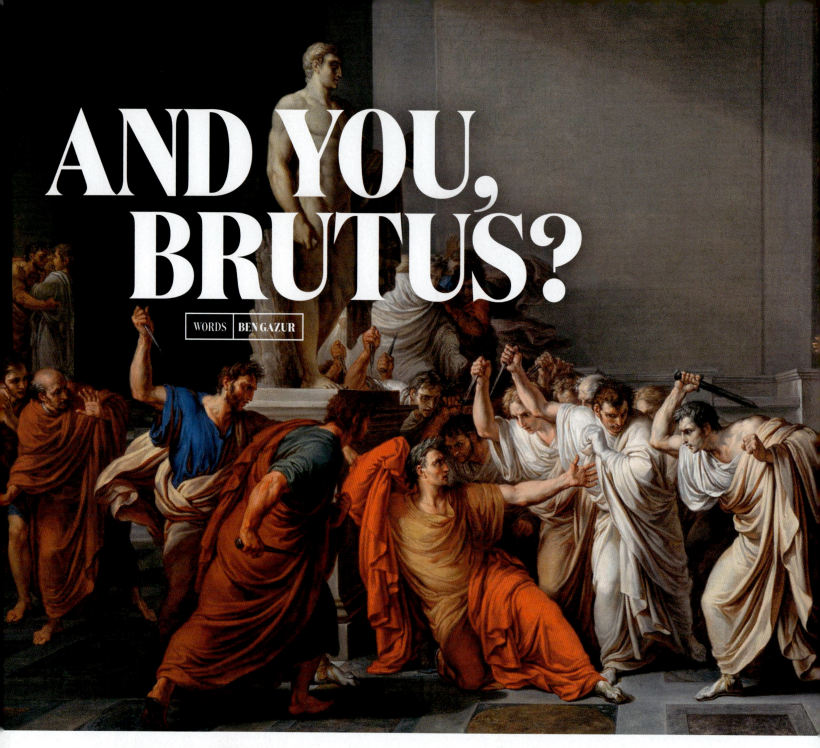

AND YOU, BRUTUS?

WORDS | BEN GAZUR

Famed for his part in the murder of Julius Caesar, was Brutus a heartless traitor or a bold liberator?

The Junia clan was among the most celebrated and important families in Rome from the earliest days of the Republic. Members of the family were routinely elected to the consulship, the highest state position, and were named dictator in times of desperation. One of the foundational legends of the Republic was a son of the Junii, Lucius Junius Brutus, had cast out the last king of Rome in the 6th century BCE and set up the constitutional order of the Republican system. When Marcus Junius Brutus, his descendent, was born in 85 BCE, there must have been high hopes that he too would rise to the peaks of power.

THE FALL OF THE REPUBLIC

In the Republican system, power was shared between the great families of the Roman patrician class through elections to various political positions and the influence of the Senate. The Republic had been designed to ensure that no one person could accumulate the total powers of a king – two consuls shared power each year and they only served for a single year. Each family competed for the honour of having the consulship, and so power tended to rotate between the families, which avoided any becoming too strong.

This system worked while Rome was a small state, but by the 1st century BCE, the Romans were beginning to govern large overseas territories. This necessitated the Republic building large armies to conquer further territories and to maintain their control of lands already taken. The generals of these mighty armies found themselves with vast military power, political influence, and incredible riches captured during campaigns. In 88 BCE, one of these commanders, Lucius Cornelius Sulla, marched on Rome to put down his political rivals and reorganise the state.

Next, Gaius Marius led his troops on the city. Each time Rome was taken, opponents of the new ruler were at risk of being killed. The zero-sum game of Roman politics had always been dangerous, but now it was literally cut-throat.

AND YOU, BRUTUS?

It was in this new world of habitual political violence that Marcus Junius Brutus was born and raised. Brutus would have known that his father had been targeted for murder by Sulla, though he managed to survive. Still, he was later killed while backing a rebellion against Sulla's supporters.

There were rumours circulating that Brutus' true father was actually someone who became one the most prominent Romans of the age – Julius Caesar. While this is unlikely given that Caesar would have been just 15 years old when Brutus was born, he was known to enjoy a close relationship with Brutus' mother, Servilia, in later life and certainly favoured Brutus when in a position of power.

THE RISE OF CAESAR AND BRUTUS

Following the civil wars of Sulla and Marius, it became clear that military might was now the true underpinning of political power. More ambitious scions of noble families focused on pursuing military commands to bolster their positions in society. One of the most successful of these was Pompey, known to history as Pompey the Great for his lightning conquests of much of the Near East. Another prominent figure, Marcus Licinius Crassus, was one of Sulla's army commanders, and he used his position to acquire an unimaginable fortune. Julius Caesar was a promising young noble but without the resources of a Pompey or Crassus. To make his way in politics he needed their support.

In 60 BCE, it was clear that the Senate was blocking Pompey from military positions he desired and Crassus from favourable financial reforms. Both had opposed the other's wishes as well due to personal rivalry. When Caesar was elected consul in 59 BCE, both, for their own political aims, supported him, and this presented an opportunity for Caesar. The three agreed to work together (a trio that became known as the First Triumvirate) to use their power to support the others in achieving their goals.

Caesar, after his consulship, was appointed to govern Gaul, and he used this position to conquer much of modern

© Getty Images, Alamy, Wikimedia Commons

RIGHT After the death of Pompey, Caesar had total control of Rome

France and enrich himself into the bargain. Caesar sent word of his daring exploits in Gaul back to Rome and lavished the population with money to win their loyalty. It was while in Gaul that he offered Brutus a position on his staff, though Brutus refused him.

Brutus launched himself onto Rome's political scene by working as an assistant to Cato, who had been appointed governor of Cyprus, and distinguishing himself for efficiency. Once back in Rome, Brutus was put in charge of the minting of new coins. A number of these were stamped with the name of Brutus, and so people would have been well familiar with him. In 53 BCE, at just 32 years of age, Brutus was elected to the Senate.

The Senate, though many members had risen due to the patronage of the Triumvirate, chafed against the influence of Caesar, Crassus and Pompey over the state. The Triumvirate began to collapse after Crassus was killed in a war against the Parthians and Caesar's daughter Julia, wife of Pompey, died. It became clear that either Caesar or Pompey would rule and sides had to be chosen. Brutus had long opposed Pompey, perhaps remembering how he had slain his father, but when Caesar marched on Rome with his Gallic legions, he sided with Pompey as the legitimate representative of the Republic.

A bloody campaign between Caesar and Pompey ended with Caesar as the sole authority in Rome and Pompey dead – along with many senators close to

FAR RIGHT Dante banished Brutus and Cassius to the deepest level of hell in his *Divine Comedy*

RIGHT Caesar's domination of Rome came through the support of his legions

BELOW Brutus issued coins with the daggers used to slay Caesar on them

ABOVE After Caesar's death the assassins sought popular support. They never received it

AND YOU, BRUTUS?

Brutus. Brutus was pardoned after the climactic battle of the civil war, and according to Plutarch, Caesar was overjoyed at his survival and made him one of his honoured friends.

THE IDES OF MARCH

In 44 BCE, Caesar made himself dictator for life, with wide-ranging powers to safeguard the Republic. Brutus may have accepted clemency from Caesar's hand but he did not subjugate himself entirely to the new order. Brutus divorced his wife and married the daughter of Cato, one of Caesar's most vocal critics. Yet, despite potentially positioning himself in opposition to Caesar, the dictator selected Brutus to serve in high office.

The Romans held the word 'king' to be an affront to everything they held dear about their Republic. Though Caesar did not proclaim himself to be king, the Romans could not but help notice he held all the powers of a king. Graffiti began to appear in public that seemed to call for Caesar to be assassinated. The statue of Brutus' ancestor, the Brutus who had driven the last king from Rome, had "O that we had thee now, Brutus!" scrawled on it, and notes were left for Brutus asking if he was asleep. Clearly, there was some appetite for freeing Rome from Caesar.

A conspiracy began to form among senators who longed for the old days when they had the power and did not serve at the command of Caesar. It is not certain who started the conspiracy, but it soon coalesced around Brutus due to his influence and the power of his name. It would be most fitting if a Brutus were to drive another 'king' out of Rome.

Soon as many as 60 senators joined the plot, and it was decided that they would strike at a meeting of the Senate on 15 March – the Ides of March. When Caesar entered he was surrounded and struck repeatedly with blows from daggers that the conspirators – or liberators, as they preferred to call themselves – had concealed in their togas. Caesar was stabbed 23 times. Legend has it that when Caesar saw Brutus in the crowd surrounding him he said, "You too, child?" (The infamous line "Et tu, Brute?" that has been attributed to Caesar comes from Shakespeare's play *Julius Caesar*.) Caesar died at the feet of a statue of his great rival, Pompey the Great.

AFTERMATH

With Caesar dead Brutus stepped forward to address the Senate – but the senators who had not been involved in the conspiracy fled the scene in disarray. When the conspirators marched through the streets with their bloody daggers to announce the return of the Republic, the people watched them in silence. It was clear that there was to be no uprising of popular support for what had been done.

Perhaps people realised that the death of Caesar was not an end to political instability. The conspirators had decided to kill Caesar alone and not all of his supporters. Mark Antony, one of Caesar's military lieutenants, could call on Caesar's legions to serve him, and so yet another civil war loomed, and it promised to be a brutal conflict.

Brutus fled east to raise money and armies to oppose Antony and Caesar's adopted son, Octavian. At the Battle of Philippi in 42 BCE, the forces of Brutus were destroyed by Antony and Octavian, and Brutus committed suicide. The other conspirators were hunted down as Antony and Octavian divided the Roman world between them. Of course, as had been proved again and again, two men could not share power forever. After one last civil war, Octavian, renamed Augustus, triumphed over Antony, marking the birth of the Roman Empire.

For his role in the death of Caesar, Brutus was seen by some as a champion of freedom, but others have viewed him as the ultimate traitor. When Dante described the lowest levels of Hell, he depicted the worst traitors in history being chewed in the jaws of Satan. Beside Judas, he placed Brutus and Cassius, the assassins of Caesar.

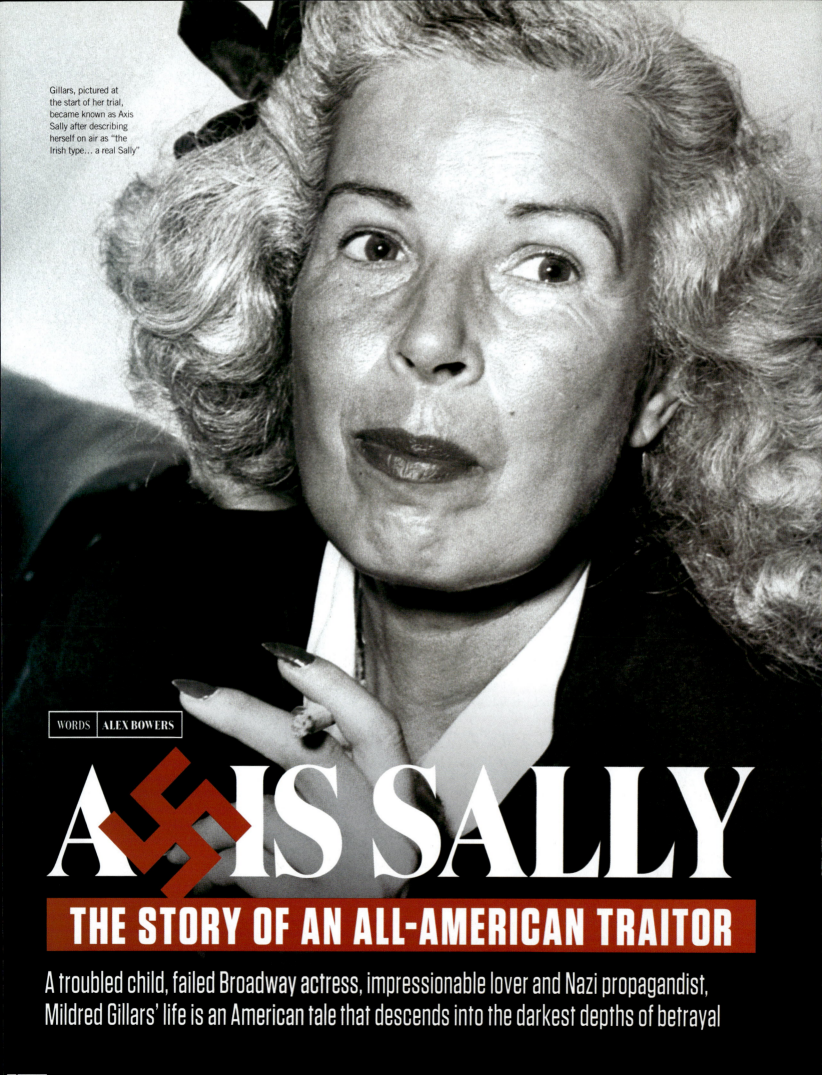

Gillars, pictured at the start of her trial, became known as Axis Sally after describing herself on air as "the Irish type… a real Sally"

WORDS | ALEX BOWERS

AXIS SALLY
THE STORY OF AN ALL-AMERICAN TRAITOR

A troubled child, failed Broadway actress, impressionable lover and Nazi propagandist, Mildred Gillars' life is an American tale that descends into the darkest depths of betrayal

AXIS SALLY

Mildred Gillars is a name synonymous with treason in the United States. During World War II the American became a broadcaster in Nazi Germany, tasked with devastating the morale of U.S. troops. Yet despite her minimal impact on America's fighting spirit, Gillars – dubbed Axis Sally by her listeners – today boasts a legacy comparable to defector Benedict Arnold, spies Julius and Ethel Rosenberg, and double-agent Robert Hanssen.

However, exactly how and why the failed actress descended from the Broadway stage and onto the fascist airwaves of the Third Reich still largely remains unexplained. "Even now, mystery and ambiguity shroud her troubled life. Many, many questions surrounding her choices remain unanswered and, frankly, probably unanswerable," Professor Michael Flamm, a scholar of modern American political history at Ohio Wesleyan University (where Gillars studied before the war), told *History of War*.

A TROUBLED CHILDHOOD

Born on 29 November 1900, Mildred Elizabeth Sisk was the daughter of Canadian parents Mary (Mae), a seamstress, and Vincent, an alcoholic blacksmith. Her early years were spent across the border in Portland, Maine, where she bore witness to her father's drunken tirades and abusive behaviour. Eventually, her mother divorced Vincent and remarried dentist Robert Bruce Gillars, also an alcoholic, whose surname Mildred took. After the birth of her half-sister Edna in 1909, the family moved to settle in Ohio.

"She was drawn to the limelight in high school, where she developed an intense interest in theatre… at Ohio Wesleyan, she essentially majored in theatre," Professor Flamm says. It was there that she likewise discovered her interest in men. As Gillars' grades slipped and her mother's second marriage deteriorated, she turned her attention to Charles M. Newcomb, a professor at Ohio Wesleyan who convinced her to abandon her studies and pursue a stage career. Dropping out of university a few credits short of her degree, she signed up for an acting school in Cleveland, accompanied by Newcomb.

THE FAILED BROADWAY ACTRESS

Once she left acting school, and with her relationship with Newcomb having run its course, Gillars remained intent on becoming a Broadway actress. From 1923, the penniless wannabe thespian tried desperately to obtain auditions, receiving the odd role or job over the next decade but failing to gain the renown she desired. A brief stint in Paris did little to kick-start her career. Disillusioned, she returned to New York City in 1929 as the Wall Street Crash decimated the creative arts industry.

"Mildred… had no family safety net to fall back upon," explains Professor Flamm. "She depended on herself. She found men who were willing to take care of her, but she also had to pursue a career because she had to pay the

Axis Sally's mugshot, taken in 1949 as she stood trial for treason

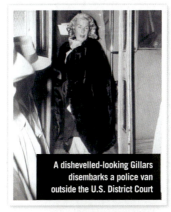

A dishevelled-looking Gillars disembarks a police van outside the U.S. District Court

While Gillars denied knowledge of the Jewish plight in Nazi Germany, she was there to witness Kristallnacht (The Night of Broken Glass) in 1938

Seen here leaving court after the first day of her trial, Gillars maintained her innocence throughout the proceedings and beyond

"NOW THE FIRST FEMALE HOST OF A MUSICAL VARIETY PROGRAMME ON THE EUROPEAN SERVICE, GILLARS WAS MAKING HER DREAM OF FAME A REALITY"

Much of Axis Sally's venomous airtime was committed to disparaging President Franklin D. Roosevelt, the British and Jewish people

rent and put food on the table and buy clothes… She had no one… who was going to provide for her." This changed when Bernard Metz, a British Jew, caught Gillars' eye. In 1932, she departed the United States to join Metz in Algiers, where he worked as a diplomat at the British Consulate.

A FRESH START… IN NAZI GERMANY

As with Newcomb, Gillars' relationship with Metz cooled. Her next fateful decision – to reunite with her mother in Europe – would see the pair visit Nazi Germany in 1934. Here Gillars would stay, in time becoming fluent in the language, studying piano and landing several jobs through a well-placed local contact. The 1936 Berlin Olympics left an impression on Gillars, although she later suggested that the games had been tainted by the "Jewish pestilence". Whether she harboured these anti-Semitic views beforehand is open to speculation.

In 1940, with World War II raging, another contact elevated Gillars to a position at Reichsradio, a broadcasting corporation that had already started bombarding the Allies with Nazi propaganda. Her initial role was limited to station identification, as well as introducing musical performances and records, yet her natural talent and charisma prompted a promotion within three months. Now the first female host of a musical variety programme on the European Service, Mildred was finally making her dream of fame a reality.

THE IMPRESSIONABLE LOVER

Max Otto Koischwitz, a German scholar, former U.S. emigrant, married man, Reichsradio producer and fervent Nazi, would set Gillars on a trajectory from which she couldn't turn back – even if she'd wanted to. The ex-actress-turned-broadcaster, having reportedly lost a prospective husband on the Eastern Front without receiving a wedding proposal, saw in Koischwitz boundless opportunities.

"On the one hand, [Koischwitz] is a master manipulator, someone who knew what strings to pull, what buttons to push, knew how to navigate Mildred towards greater and greater stardom to the point where she becomes the highest-paid performer on Reichsradio," says Professor Flamm. "He also fits the profile throughout her life: Mildred was attracted to older men who were frequently inaccessible or unavailable, at least in terms of being married and already having families."

Her dependence on Koischwitz reached new heights on 7 December 1941, when Japan attacked Pearl Harbor. Professor Flamm continues: "It's vital to remember that Mildred is effectively trapped in Germany after [the Japanese attack]… [Months earlier] in the fall of 1941, Mildred was summoned to the U.S. embassy in Berlin and told to return to the United States… Mildred refused… she was finally enjoying a measure of celebrity and financial security… The U.S. embassy takes away her passport, so she can't travel… Could she have gone back to the U.S. embassy and pleaded her case? That's a possible scenario. But perhaps in her mind she had burned her bridges with the U.S."

THE NAZI PROPAGANDIST

To stave off enemy alien status, Gillars signed a loyalty oath to Nazi Germany. "At that point," says Professor Flamm, "her destiny was set." Entirely under the influence of Koischwitz, Gillars was steered towards propaganda. In 1942, as American GIs embarked on Operation Torch in North Africa, she became the star of Home Sweet Home, a musical programme with political commentary designed to make American personnel feel homesick. The show opened with the classic American sound of a train whistle, played American jazz and swing music, and featured Gillars – under the name Midge – in a seductive American voice. Her broadcasts attempted to spread doubt about the validity of the Allied cause and even alluded to unfaithful wives and girlfriends back in the States. Soldiers at the front who tuned in rarely called her Midge, preferring instead the Berlin Bitch or Axis Sally.

Much to Gillars' disdain, she would be joined by another Axis Sally, an Italian-American called Rita Luisa Zucca. Furthermore, a Japanese counterpart known as Tokyo Rose – real name Iva Toguri D'Aquino, a Japanese-American – shared in the infamy. Together with defected British broadcasters such as William Joyce, better known as Lord Haw-Haw, they sometimes had the power to ominously and often accurately describe Allied positions, their seemingly all-knowing voices unnerving listeners who had thought their movements were secret.

BELOW These American soldiers have tuned in to hear news of President Roosevelt's death, but many of them may previously have heard Axis Sally's broadcasts

The defence attorney James J. Laughlin (centre) would face off against the prosecution's lawyer, John Kelley, who eventually won over the grand jury

"AMERICAN PRISONERS RECOGNISED GILLARS' VOICE, REFUSED TO PARTICIPATE AND HURLED INSULTS AS SHE LEFT"

Martin James Monti, who had a short stint at Axis Sally's broadcasting station against her wishes, had defected to Nazi Germany in a stolen P-38 aircraft

Axis Sally desired fame but received infamy and a 12-year jail sentence instead

Edna Gillars (right) remained supportive of her half-sister, even after Axis Sally was found guilty of treason

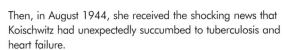

Battling Axis forces and the fierce heat of North Africa, American troops involved in Operation Torch became all too familiar with Gillars' radio persona

Gillars was temporarily released for Christmas 1946. However, the furore it caused at home prompted her re-arrest and return to jail

Christmas 1942 saw Gillars' and Koischwitz's bond change from colleagues to lovers – and with it the transition from down-on-her-luck actress to Nazi mouthpiece was complete. "Mildred pretty consistently argued [on air] that there was some sort of Jewish, Bolshevik or communist conspiracy to destroy the civilised world and that, in fact, the Nazis were doing the world a favour by fighting the Soviets," says Professor Flamm. "But sometimes she also mixed in an anti-British message… that perhaps the British somehow lured the United States into war [against Germany] for their own interests, for the empire."

Combined with her widely broadcasted hatred for U.S. President Franklin Roosevelt, she had all the makings of an American traitor.

THE TIGHTENING NOOSE

Axis Sally's stardom increased, including a show entitled *Midge at the Mike*, which reached out as far as North America to target mothers and partners of soldiers. But Koischwitz was keeping a secret from his mistress: it turned out that his wife was pregnant with their fourth child. When Gillars learned of the infant she attempted to take her own life. Tragically, it would be Koischwitz's newborn who died after just a few hours. Nine days later Koischwitz's wife was killed in an Allied air raid that hit the hospital.

The radio-personality couple would nevertheless continue their lives together, both on and off air. With the tide of the war changing, Gillars' most notorious broadcast, 'Vision of Invasion', aired in May 1944, a drama in which she played an Ohio mother foreseeing her son's death in a failed D-Day attempt. Additionally, Axis Sally arranged to interview Allied POWs at camps, editing their words to conform to propaganda angles and reporting – in borderline sadistic detail – the afflictions of the wounded to highlight the terrible cost of conflict. In one instance, a group of American prisoners recognised Gillars' voice, refused to participate and hurled insults as she left. Gillars began posing as an International Red Cross representative to achieve her goals.

Then, in August 1944, she received the shocking news that Koischwitz had unexpectedly succumbed to tuberculosis and heart failure.

The noose was tightening around Axis Sally. Deluded into believing that she had done nothing wrong, she disassociated herself with fellow American traitor Martin James Monti, who, having defected from the U.S. military, had joined Reichsradio in early 1945. Gillars deemed him guilty of treason while thinking she was innocent. It mattered little, though, as Nazi Germany was about to lose the war – and Gillars was a wanted woman.

THE TRIAL OF AXIS SALLY

A fugitive in her adopted country for 11 months, Gillars was captured in the British Sector of Berlin on 15 March 1946. Upon her arrest she requested to take only one item with her: a photograph of her beloved Koischwitz. Axis Sally spent two years in an Allied internment camp, without charges or legal representation, until her extradition to the United States in 1948. Her subsequent trial would bring to light numerous moral conundrums associated with the proceedings, not least whether words constituted a treasonous act against the United States of America.

"It wasn't a fair trial," says Professor Flamm. "[The defence] had very limited resources. The Federal Government made no witnesses available to the defence who could have testified to the very real threat of arrest and deportation that Mildred faced. In other words, bringing up the idea that she was coerced into making this broadcast…"

Nor did Axis Sally help her own case, as Professor Flamm explains: "Mildred takes the stand [and] damages her credibility. She denies it was her voice on the radio, she refused to express any remorse for her actions… She always claimed that she knew nothing about the Holocaust, that she knew nothing about the fate of the Jews and would not apologise. And she made the point that she was an artist, not a propagandist. That, by the way, is an interesting thing to consider… [the] First Amendment [argument]: 'I'm an artist. This is my freedom of expression.' That's an interesting legal argument that wasn't fully pursued.

"Ultimately, Mildred was convicted on only one of the eight charges of treason. And that single charge was based on a radio drama… a 'Vision of Invasion', in which Mildred was, in fact, reading from a script… There was no free-form political commentary." It would still be enough for her to face 12 years in prison.

THE LEGACY OF AN AMERICAN TRAITOR

Gillars remained unapologetic for the rest of her life, even after her 1961 release, when she converted to Catholicism and became a teacher at an Ohio convent. In 1973, she finally completed her degree. She died of colon cancer on 25 June 1988, aged 87.

Remarking on her legacy and whether Axis Sally was a victim of her lover's influence, Professor Flamm says: "Personally, I do not believe that Koischwitz was entirely the string puller or puppet master. I believe that Mildred has a substantial degree of responsibility. Her life patterns suggest she made choices and decisions, and she had to live with the consequences…

"Axis Sally today is a footnote in history… I doubt that in the future we will see many treason trials based on political propaganda or commentary given the scepticism about truths and facts in our world today."

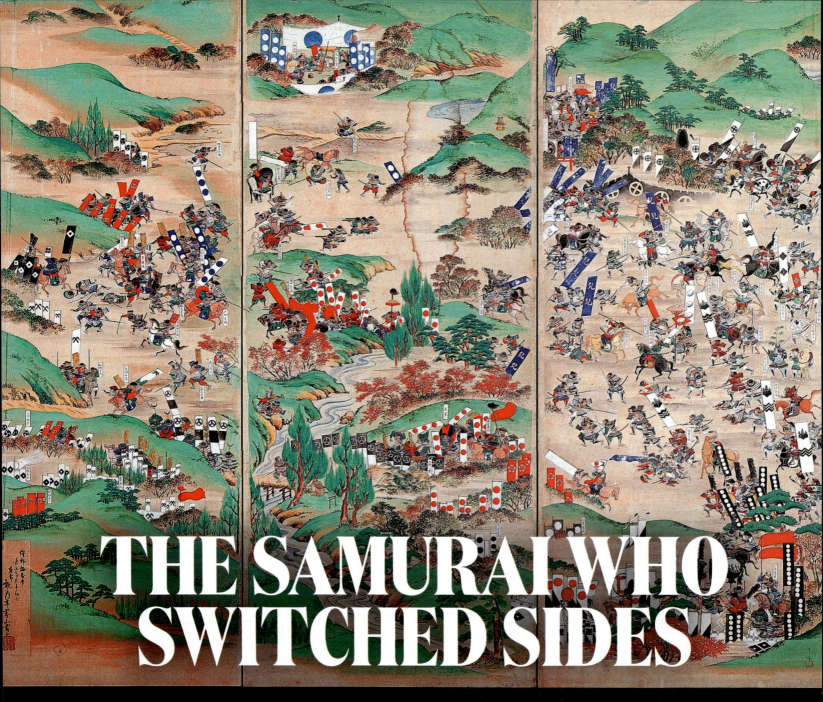

THE SAMURAI WHO SWITCHED SIDES

Kobayakawa Hideaki's lust for revenge changed the course of Japanese history

WORDS | SCOTT REEVES

Nineteenth February 1598 should have been the greatest day of Kobayakawa Hideaki's life. The samurai warlord was part of a relief force that came to the rescue of a besieged Japanese garrison at Tosan Fortress in Korea. Kobayakawa was in the thick of the action, leading a charge and forcing the enemy to retreat. He wielded a spear, cut down opponents and directed his troops to capture an enemy commander. Thanks to Kobayakawa's intervention, the beleaguered garrison was saved.

Unfortunately for Kobayakawa, his bravery only helped the Japanese to make the best of a bad situation. The Japanese invasion of Korea was already failing. The government back home was fragile and facing the prospect of civil war, and they didn't take kindly to Kobayakawa's heroics on the front line.

Kobayakawa expected praise for his role in saving Tosan Fortress. Instead, his superiors chastised him for leading a reckless charge and putting himself in harm's way. As far as they were concerned, Kobayakawa's job was to command, not to lead from the front. They decided to make an example of him. Rather than rewarding Kobayakawa for his efforts, he was stripped of his lands, flung in prison and threatened with execution.

Eight months later, when emotions had cooled, Kobayakawa was released and had his lands reinstated. Only now, he had a chip on his shoulder – and he focused his resentment on one person: Ishida Mitsunari, the samurai who'd led the scathing criticism of Kobayakawa's charge. Kobayakawa began plotting revenge on the man he blamed for his fall from grace.

Two years later, Kobayakawa got his chance to settle the score. Japan slipped into another civil war as the government faced off against the Tokugawa clan from the East. Mitsunari took command of the loyalist Western Army with orders to subdue the rebels – and among Mitsunari's subordinate commanders was the rehabilitated but resentful Kobayakawa Hideaki.

At first, all seemed well. Kobayakawa followed Mitsunari's orders and helped to capture Fushimi Castle after a ten-day siege. Mitsunari was pleased that the previously gung-ho Kobayakawa now seemed to be a model underling. But Kobayakawa was merely biding his

THE SAMURAI WHO SWITCHED SIDES

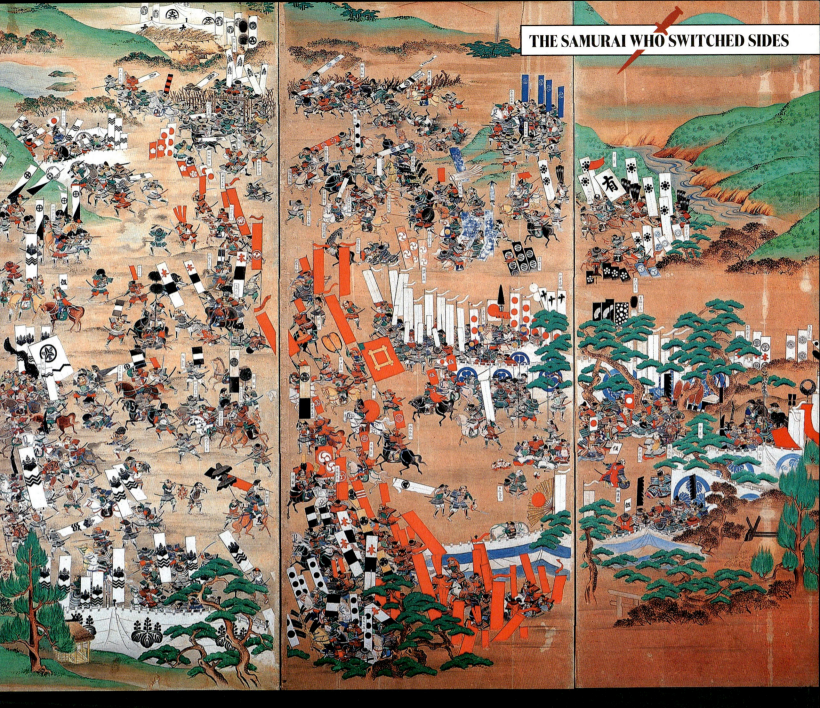

time. He realised that Fushimi Castle was going to fall no matter what, and he used the assault to get back into Mitsunari's confidence.

Six weeks later, the Western and Eastern armies stumbled across each other in heavy fog just outside Sekigahara. Since the Western forces easily outnumbered the Eastern rebels, Mitsunari expected that the forthcoming battle would deal a knockout blow. But Mitsunari had no idea that he had a traitor in his midst.

According to the traditional telling of the tale, Kobayakawa held secret talks about switching sides before the battle began, but he was still uncommitted when the fighting started. To spur him into action, Eastern cannons fired blanks at Kobayakawa's ranks to prove they could wipe out his men if he didn't defect. That forced Kobayakawa's hand, and he led a charge against the rest of the unsuspecting Western Army.

The story that Eastern cannons persuaded Kobayakawa to switch sides may be more fiction than fact. Instead, many modern historians suspect that Kobayakawa defected as soon as the battle began – but whenever he turned traitor, the result was the same.

> "KOBAYAKAWA BEGAN PLOTTING REVENGE ON THE MAN HE BLAMED FOR HIS FALL FROM GRACE"

Kobayakawa's double-cross caused one flank of the Western Army to crumble, and this spurred four other samurai to change sides and fight for the rebels.

The armies were now evenly matched, but the momentum favoured the East. By early afternoon, the Western Army was on the run. Upwards of 30,000 Western soldiers were killed. Mitsunari fled the battlefield but was captured and executed less than two weeks later.

In the days following the battle, the man whose betrayal caused Mitsunari's downfall rubbed salt in the wounds. Kobayakawa led his troops to Mitsunari's home castle, less than a day's march from the battlefield. The castle's garrison had been almost completely stripped for the battle, and it fell to Kobayakawa in just half a day. In the aftermath, Kobayakawa killed most of Mitsunari's surviving relatives to ensure the death of his bloodline.

The Battle of Sekigahara may be best known for Kobayakawa's betrayal, but it had wider consequences than sating his desire for revenge. It also marked the end of the Sengoku period and the beginning of the Tokugawa shogunate, a new dynasty that would rule Japan for the next 250 years.

ONCE, TWICE, THREE TIMES A TRAITOR

Mir Jafar's lust for power made him betray his people, his allies and his family

WORDS | SCOTT REEVES

Mir Jafar left his mark on Indian history on 23 June 1757 – remembered as Bengal's day of infamy. At first glance, it should have been an easy victory. An army of 50,000 men representing Nawab Siraj ud-Daulah of Bengal had cornered 3,000 soldiers from the British East India Company at Plassey, around 160 kilometres (100 miles) north of Calcutta. But the Bengalis had a traitor in their ranks.

For over a century, the East India Company had been taking advantage of the gradual disintegration of the Mughal Empire in India. British merchants wheedled their way into India, making lucrative deals and taking control of political institutions, often at the point of a gun. The conflict escalated in 1756 when war broke out between Britain and France, and fighting spread into their imperial interests in Asia. The Nawab of Bengal (modern-day Bangladesh) tried to maintain his independence by aligning with the French and seizing control of the Company-ruled city of Calcutta – but the East India Company wasn't about to let him.

The crisis came to a head at Plassey. The two armies exchanged artillery fire for hours until a heavy rainstorm dampened the cannons. Nawab Siraj took the opportunity to order a cavalry charge, but his commander was killed. Sensing that the conditions didn't favour his army, the Nawab ordered his forces to withdraw into entrenchments. But the left flank of his army lingered behind the rest. That section was led by Mir Jafar, the Nawab's principal general and the army's paymaster, an officer whose loyalty had been questioned over recent months. The sceptics had good reason to doubt Jafar's allegiance.

Jafar had never been satisfied with the Nawab's leadership, and he was willing to contemplate an alternative ruler taking charge – ideally himself. So Jafar listened when the British offered him substantial bribes and a promise of power if he helped to overthrow Nawab Siraj. By May 1757, it was agreed. Jafar joined the Nawab's campaign against the British, but he was secretly working against him.

The British were aware that Jafar was a slippery character, and they doubted whether he'd go through with the plot. Only by mid-afternoon at the Battle of Plassey, around seven hours after the first shots were fired, did it become clear that Jafar's division wasn't following the Nawab's orders to entrench. Instead, it was marching away from the battlefield, leaving the Nawab's flank completely exposed. Soon, the British rained artillery fire on the Bengali troops from higher ground that Jafar had left exposed.

Although losses on both sides were relatively low – the British suffered 77 casualties, the Bengalis around 500 – the British had the momentum. The Nawab went on the run, and the day after the battle, the British hailed Jafar as the new Nawab of Bengal. When Nawab Siraj was captured Jafar had him killed.

Mir Jafar was now the undisputed ruler of Bengal, but unlike the previous nawab, Jafar was far from independent. He wanted to be feted as an equal of the East India Company. Instead, he was a subordinate. He signed a treaty granting the East India Company extended lands and trading rights in Bengal. Jafar also had to pay a vast amount of compensation to the British, but Nawab Siraj left behind an empty treasury, and Jafar fell behind on the payments almost immediately.

It didn't take long for Jafar's treasonous side to rear its head again. Within two years he began secret negotiations with the Dutch, asking them to expel the British from Bengal. The Dutch sent seven ships and 1,400 men under the pretence of reinforcing the Dutch trading post at Chinsurah. The British responded with a force that intercepted the Dutch, and in the battle that followed they captured every one of the Dutch ships. Jafar claimed ignorance of the Dutch plans, but the British weren't fooled. They deposed Jafar from the throne and replaced him with his nephew, Mir Qasim.

Jafar still wasn't finished with his plotting. His last chance to double-cross came when Qasim fell out of favour with the British. The East India Company launched a military operation against Qasim and deposed him after four years as nawab. His replacement was none other than Jafar, who'd talked his way back into the British good books, even at the expense of double-crossing his own family.

Jafar's second time on the throne didn't last long. He died in February 1765, little more than a year later, leaving behind a reputation as a traitor whose willingness to betray his own people led to two centuries of British domination.

DENMARK'S GREATEST TRAITOR

When he married into the Danish royal family, Corfitz Ulfeldt had it all. So what made him decide to betray king and country by serving Denmark's mortal foe?

WORDS | CATHERINE CURZON

Count Corfitz Ulfeldt was born to privilege in 1606, and from the moment of his birth, his was a life that was destined for noble things. He was the son of Jacob Ulfeldt, chancellor to King Christian IV of Denmark and grandson of one of the country's privy councillor. The Ulfeldt family were loyal, influential and trusted by the House of Oldenburg. After generations of faithful service, one of the Ulfeldts was the last person anyone would expect to turn traitor.

As one might expect of someone with such an illustrious pedigree, no expense was spared on educating Corfitz Ulfeldt and preparing him for the life that awaited. In fact, so close to the ruling house were the Ulfeldts that, when King Christian VI's daughter, Leonora Christina, was born in 1621, there was only one choice for a future husband. She was just nine years old when she was betrothed to the 24-year-old Corfitz, an illustrious future mapped out for both. It must have been a proud moment indeed for the Ulfeldt family, their years of faithful service finally repaid by semi-admission into the royal family they had so loyally worked for through the generations.

Leonora Christina, however, was not actually a royal princess. Instead, she was the daughter of Christian IV's second wife, Kirsten Munk, who would bear the king 12 children. As a noble rather than a royal, the marriage was morganatic, meaning that Leonora Christina could only take the title of countess. Despite this she was still recognised as a daughter of the king, and that brought with it a certain status regardless of who her mother was.

With his future marriage taken care of, Ulfeldt's formative years were spent learning the ways of the Danish court and political world, and he finished his education in Italy under the guidance of the great philosopher Cesare Cremonini before returning home.

He swiftly settled into life as a courtier and won the trust of King Christian IV. Count Ulfeldt's rise through the ranks was swift, and just as his career was in the ascendance, so too was his personal life. Ulfeldt was appointed governor of Copenhagen in 1637, the same year that he married his 16-year-old royal bride. This was no love match, though, but one of vital dynastic importance to the future of Denmark.

Although the Oldenburgs had ruled Denmark since 1448, this was not a typical hereditary monarchy and no son was granted the right of automatic succession until he had been elected by the Rigsraadet. This body, which translates as the Council of the State, was a council of Danish nobles who served as councillors to the monarchy, placing checks and balances on each king in order to ensure that no sovereign could abuse his power. It was the members of the Rigsraadet who were responsible for formally electing the next in the line of succession once the Danish king died, and each time they did so they introduced new challenges to his powers.

Bit by bit, king by king, the Rigsraadet chipped away at the monarch's power. Yet by marrying his children to

ABOVE LEFT Ulfeldt and Leonora Christina were betrothed when she was just a child, yet they proved to be very well-matched

ABOVE RIGHT Charles X Gustav of Sweden was sure that his Swedish army could easily take Denmark. He was badly mistaken

members of the council, Christian IV cannily ensured that he was tying in at least some measure of loyalty. After all, as a son-in-law to the king, a council member might be less likely to impose too many sanctions on a new monarch, and Christian married six of his children to Rigsraadet representatives, hoping to secure the loyalty of each new husband. In the case of Corfitz Ulfeldt, of course, King Christian IV was fatally mistaken.

Ulfeldt's rise had been swift and his ambition was boundless, yet it was not always matched by ability. He was a ruthless but not a particularly talented strategist, and his faults were laid bare for all to see when he was given a command in the war between Denmark and Sweden that broke out in 1643. By now appointed to the powerful position of steward of the realm, Ulfeldt commanded Danish troops as they marched into Sweden from Norwegian territory. The attempted invasion was thwarted and Ulfeldt's troops were given no choice but to retreat. Ulfeldt was given a second chance to prove himself when he was charged with negotiating the Second Treaty of Brömsebro on behalf of Denmark, which was intended to reach a peaceful outcome between Sweden and Denmark-Norway.

In truth, there was little that Ulfeldt could have negotiated for Denmark, for his nation was completely outgunned by its Swedish opponents. Yet by any standards the cost to Denmark was high, resulting in vast and sweeping territorial losses. Christian IV blamed Ulfeldt for the defeat and subsequent embarrassment to Denmark, and the two men almost came to blows after a furious confrontation. Yet the king knew that he could not afford to alienate his son-in-law and refused to accept Ulfeldt's resignation. Instead, he appointed him to a new position as ambassador, a role at which Ulfeldt far from excelled. Instead he lived a life of pomp and circumstance, enjoying the best of everything while achieving very little that the king had expected.

Yet Christian couldn't risk incurring the wrath of Ulfeldt and, potentially, his noble allies in the Rigsraadet. After all, if there was one thing that the Danish sovereigns knew, it was that their councillors must be kept on side. As steward of the realm, no noble was more important that Ulfeldt, with the title conferring on him the powers that one might better associate with a prime minister. It was an office that would prove fateful for Ulfeldt.

In February 1648, Christian IV of Denmark died and left his son and heir, Frederick III, to inherit the crown. Of course, the Danish succession was not complete until the Rigsraadet had elected the new king, and this was subject to even more discussion than usual. Frederick had already caused some discomfort among the nobles after difficult forays into leadership, and the members of the Rigsraadet

> "THE KING COULDN'T RISK INCURRING THE WRATH OF ULFELDT AND, POTENTIALLY, HIS NOBLE ALLIES"

DENMARK'S GREATEST TRAITOR

The traitor's queen
FROM CHILD BRIDE TO PRISONER TO NATIONAL HEROINE, LEONORA CHRISTINA WASN'T A TYPICAL HISTORICAL HEROINE

When she and her husband were arrested, Leonora Christina refused to speak out against Ulfeldt. Though he was able to escape, she remained in custody, forced to watch as he was burned in effigy. Kept in prison, Leonora Christina made no efforts to escape, not did she lower herself to beg for her freedom.

Without being charged with any crime or subject to any trial, she remained a prisoner in the Blue Tower for 22 years. Conditions were harsh and she shared her dirty cell with rats, yet she wouldn't allow her voice to be silenced. She seized every scrap of paper she could find, no matter how meagre, and used the charred end of her quill to write. She eventually developed an odd camaraderie with the rats that infested her cell. She wrote of their behaviour and studied them closely, finding them better company than the wardens who treated her with cruelty, subjecting her to their unwanted advances.

When Frederick III died his successor, Christian V, improved her conditions somewhat, but his mother refused to grant him permission to free Leonora Christina. Under this new regime she was moved to more comfortable surroundings and was allowed books and writing materials.

When she was finally freed at the age of 63, Leonora Christina made her home at Maribo Monastery, where she wrote voraciously. Here she put her prison writings in order and composed accounts of her years in captivity, as well as the dazzling times she had known before her imprisonment. She became an icon of female endurance, a woman who refused to bow down and who, upon hearing of her husband's death, did not mourn nor lament her own captivity. Instead she rejoiced, delighted that he had evaded his enemies to the very end.

Through her memoirs Leonora Christina became famous, and when she died in 1698 she left behind a rich literary legacy as both a writer and translator. To this day she is remembered as a heroine of Scandinavian history.

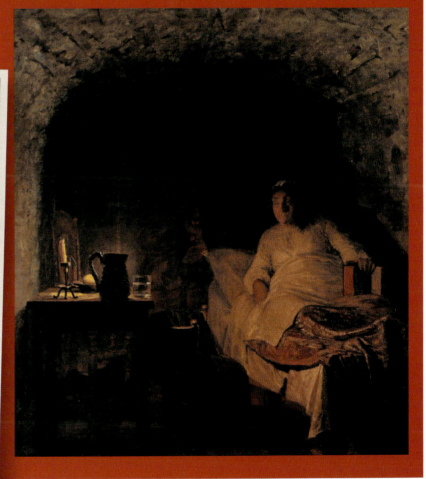

LEFT Betrayed by Ulfeldt, King Frederick III of Denmark longed for revenge

OPPOSITE Leonora Christina grew up in the shadow of the tower that would one day become her prison

did not intend to elect him unopposed. While the throne of Denmark remained unoccupied the natural caretaker leader was, of course, Ulfeldt, the steward of the realm.

Together, Ulfeldt and Leonora Christina ruled over Denmark as though they were king and queen. As Frederick seethed in the wings, awaiting his moment on the stage, his resentment of Ulfeldt grew. He saw not a statesman at the helm of a rudderless ship but a man of ambition and limitless intrigue desperate to usurp the power of the monarchy and encourage his fellow nobles to limit Frederick's powers to the point that he was virtually a figurehead. By the time the new king began his reign he was determined to rid himself of this troublesome noble.

Frederick III decided to audit the financial affairs of his ministers and among them, of course, was Count Ulfeldt.

The reign of Frederick III

FREDERICK III WAS DETERMINED TO NEUTER ULFELDT, BUT WHAT BECAME OF THE KING?

Frederick III didn't like Corfitz Ulfeldt, but the people of Denmark loved Frederick III. After all, he stood firm against the invasion of Charles X Gustav's forces literally and figuratively, forcing the Swedes to abandon their efforts despite the odds being heavily stacked against the Danes. After his defeat in the Dano-Swedish War of 1657–58, when the 1658–59 war broke out, the king was determined that this time he would not be beaten.

In an unheard of turn of events, Frederick invited Charles X Gustav, who was determined to conquer Denmark, to spend a few days as his guest in Copenhagen. The two men got on famously, but Charles was not about to let friendship interfere with his plans for conquest. Yet Frederick now quite literally knew his enemy and he was determined not to let Copenhagen fall. When the moment came to defend the capital the Danes rallied to their king's call and forced the Swedish forces back with the assistance of a Dutch naval fleet. Denmark ultimately emerged from the conflict victorious.

Frederick capitalised on his popularity, and this time those nobles who had once sought to control the monarch were possessed with a blind loyalty. Dazzled by Frederick's showing against Sweden and taken in by his expert handling of politics, they put up no objection when he moved to introduce an absolute monarchy.

For the final decade of his life Frederick III was entirely occupied by the overhaul of royal power. The face of Denmark began to change slowly but definitively and, unlike any other European absolute monarchy, the new order was supported by a constitution. The Rigsraadet, once all-powerful, was swept out of existence, ending the traditional politicking that went into the election of each new sovereign. Frederick himself had been forced to make concessions to the Rigsraadet to ensure that he was elected to his own throne. He had always felt the sting of that, so putting a final stop to the interference of the Rigsraadet was no doubt a victory that the king savoured.

DENMARK'S GREATEST TRAITOR

With allegations of financial irregularities coming to the fore, Ulfeldt's life was further complicated by a false accusation of conspiracy made by his former mistress, Dina Vinhofvers. Vinhofvers alleged that Ulfeldt was intending to poison the king and his heirs and stage a coup to take over Denmark. Ulfeldt was experienced enough to recognise which way the wind was blowing and fled Denmark with Leonora Christina, heading to the relative safety of Amsterdam.

Wanted in the land of his birth to answer difficult questions about his financial affairs, Ulfeldt had no choice but to become a fugitive. The life of luxury he and his wife had once enjoyed was nothing but a distant memory and the couple endured privations and danger to evade capture. Yet Ulfeldt's ambition and cunning served him well, and when Charles X Gustav of Sweden invaded Denmark, the steward of the realm rallied to the call of his former enemy. He was motivated entirely by personal malice and the desire for revenge against Frederick III, who had brought about his disgrace and downfall, and now he intended to see Sweden crush the land that he had once served and to get rich all over again in the process.

Ulfeldt became Sweden's loudest champion. With the money he had stolen during his Danish reign he was able to finance the armies of his homeland's mortal enemy, and his insider knowledge was priceless to his new Swedish paymasters. As a member of the Swedish army, he led troops into Denmark, standing shoulder to shoulder with Charles X Gustav as the Swedish king crushed the Danes. In a final insult, he presided over the Treaty of Taastrup and the humiliation of the land that his ancestors had been so loyal to.

Yet a man like Ulfeldt could never be satisfied, and though Charles X Gustav repaid him with money and titles, he was soon up to his old tricks. Just as he had undermined Frederick in Denmark, now he began to intrigue against Charles X Gustav too. This time, however, he had pushed his luck too far, and in 1659 he and his wife were thrown into prison. Sentenced to death, it seemed as though Count Ulfeldt had reached the end of the road.

Some men, it is claimed, live a charmed life, and Ulfeldt might have thought himself one of them because, two months later, the couple were released under the terms of an amnesty. The couple returned to Denmark and attempted to insinuate themselves into power once more, but it was not to be. Placed under arrest, they were subject to harsh conditions in a glowering fortress named Hammershus, a far cry from the lives they had once known. Their captivity was brutal and merciless and there was no hope of escape, but, eventually, the couple agreed to sign away all that they owned in return for their freedom.

Upon his release Ulfeldt's thoughts turned once again to revenge. He approached Frederick William I, elector of Brandenburg, offering to instigate a Danish rebellion on his behalf, but the elector knew better than to trust the by now infamous noble. Instead he told the Danish king, Frederick III, what Ulfeldt had suggested and Ulfeldt was arrested and condemned to death.

Amazingly, Ulfeldt escaped, and in his absence his effigy was pilloried, beheaded and quartered. Ulfeldt died one year later in 1664 while on board a boat on the Rhine near the city Basel. Precisely how he died remains unknown, but the body of Denmark's greatest traitor disappeared, never to be seen again.

ATHELRED'S HIRED MUSCLE

Eadric Streona's double-crossing changed the fate of England forever

| WORDS | SCOTT REEVES |

For the first few years of his career, there wasn't much sign that Eadric Streona would become Anglo-Saxon England's greatest traitor. Instead, Eadric was a loyal – albeit brutal – servant to King Athelred the Unready.

Eadric rose from relatively humble origins to play a key role in Athelred's court. Athelred was keenly aware that ruling over Anglo-Saxon England was a risky business. Various family members who descended from Alfred the Great vied for the job, and Athelred only came to the throne after his half-brother, Edward the Martyr, was assassinated. Viking raiders still threatened to overwhelm the kingdom, and generations of Danes had settled in the north.

In a court dominated with factional intrigue and machination, Eadric was Athelred's hired muscle. No job was off limits. In 1006, Eadric invited Ealdorman (or Earl) Alfhelm of York to visit his estates in Shrewsbury for a hunting trip. It was a one-way journey. Athelred doubted Alfhelm's loyalty, and Eadric arranged for him to be murdered while he was out of the sight of his bodyguards.

A few years later, when Sweyn Forkbeard invaded England and briefly seized the throne, Eadric loyally accompanied Athelred into exile on the other side of the English Channel. After Sweyn's sudden death, Eadric returned with Athelred and set about ruthlessly taking back the kingdom, punishing anybody they thought had accepted Sweyn without a fight. In 1015, Eadric accused two nobles of plotting with the Vikings and had them killed.

So important had Eadric become to Athelred's regime that he married the king's daughter and was named Ealdorman of Mercia. But Eadric sensed the tide was turning when Athelred's health began to decline in 1015. It was soon apparent that his father-in-law was dying and England would need a new king. Rather than back Athelred's son and heir, Prince Edmund, Eadric switched sides and joined Sweyn Forkbeard's son Cnut. Eadric seized 40 ships of the royal fleet and set sail for Denmark, where he was welcomed with open arms and a promise that he would remain an ealdorman under Cnut's regime.

As Athelred lay dying, Cnut invaded England, with Eadric by his side. At the Battle of Sherston, fought shortly after Athelred's death in April 1016, Eadric tried to gain the upper hand through nefarious means. He identified a man who looked similar to Prince Edmund and had his head cut off. Then Eadric held the head aloft, shouting that Edmund was dead. Unfortunately for both Eadric and Edmund's lookalike, the hoax didn't work.

For the next few weeks, the two armies shadowed and parried but with little result. Then Edmund received a surprise visitor. It was Eadric, begging forgiveness. He'd seen the error of his ways and wanted to return to Edmund's service.

The new alliance didn't last long. At the Battle of Assandun in October 1016, Edmund faced off against Cnut one more time, and Eadric played another battlefield trick. Shortly after the two armies had engaged, Eadric ordered the men under his command to flee the field, enabling Cnut's soldiers to punch through the English ranks and score a crushing victory for the Danes. Eadric hadn't returned to Edmund's side at all – it was all a ruse designed to deal a fatal blow to Edmund's kingly ambitions, and it worked.

Shortly after the Battle of Assandun, Edmund and Cnut agreed a negotiated settlement. Edmund kept Wessex while Cnut had the rest of England. Whoever lived longer would inherit the other man's kingdom after his death. It wasn't a treaty conducive to a lasting peace, and so it proved. Just a few weeks later, Edmund died suddenly.

Nobody knows exactly how Edmund passed away. It may have been a natural death, although the timing was just too convenient for Cnut. Some suggest that Edmund was stabbed or shot with an arrow while sitting on the toilet. Many of the conspiracy theorists think that the assassin was employed by Eadric, or was even Eadric himself.

At last England was at peace – or as peaceful as it got in the Anglo-Saxon era. But Cnut sat uneasily on the throne. He knew that among his retinue was a man who'd already betrayed one king and who seemed perfectly capable of doing it again. So on Christmas Day 1017, one year after seizing the throne, Cnut ordered Eadric's execution. Eadric was beheaded with a battle axe and his head was displayed on London Bridge.

Eadric's death ended the plotting of Anglo-Saxon England's most notorious turncoat, and it also meant that King Cnut slept a little safer in his bed.

ABOVE Edmund and Cnut negotiated a settlement to end their war for England, but only after Eadric's intervention

ABOVE Eadric rose to prominence serving this man, Athelred the Unready, but turned against him when Athelred was on his deathbed

ATHELRED'S HIRED MUSCLE

BELOW Eadric holds aloft the head of Osmear, a warrior who was unfortunate enough to resemble Edmund

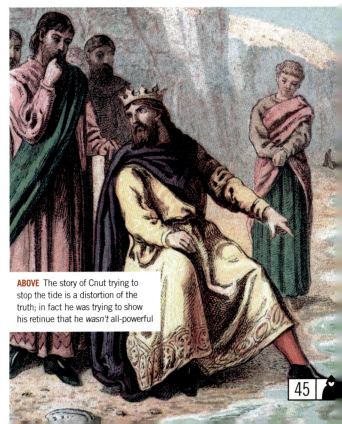

ABOVE The story of Cnut trying to stop the tide is a distortion of the truth; in fact he was trying to show his retinue that he *wasn't* all-powerful

SELLER OF STATE SECRETS

What drove a high-ranking Austro-Hungarian officer to divulge top-secret information to the enemies of the empire?

WORDS | MICHAEL E. HASKEW

Outward appearances can be deceiving, and such was the case with Alfred Redl, for years the respected and trusted head of the Evidenzbureau, the counterintelligence section of the Austro-Hungarian Army General Staff.

In service to the Habsburg monarchy, Redl was the embodiment of a dedicated military man. Born on 14 March 1864, in relative poverty in Lemberg, Galicia, in the Austrian Empire (today the city of Lviv in Ukraine) he was the son of a railway clerk and one of seven children. He embarked on a military career at the age of 15, attending the Imperial War School in Vienna before joining the army's intelligence section in 1900.

Fluent in several languages, Redl reached the rank of colonel and took charge of counterintelligence by 1907. By all appearances, he was the consummate spymaster – training his own operatives, maintaining vigilance against the perceived enemies of the Habsburgs and recognised for his prowess by friend and adversary alike. However, he lived not only a secret life, but one that was multi-faceted. Publicly, he was the picture of astuteness, but amid the shadows of political intrigue he was also a double agent selling secrets to Russia for approximately 12 years and known to his handlers there as Agent No. 25. He was probably on the payrolls of other countries as well.

When in control of Austro-Hungarian counterintelligence, Redl introduced new techniques in surveillance, information gathering and interrogation – this included the use of primitive recording devices and cameras, a fingerprinting system, and the "Third Degree" – blinding prisoners with harsh lights while bombarding them with questions.

A contemporary described Redl as "clever, reserved, concentrated and efficient. His outward appearance seems greasy. He speaks sugar-sweetly, softly, and in a servile manner. His movements are measured and slow. He is more clever and false than smart and talented. A cynic...."

What was it, then, that caused Redl to turn traitor? It was no secret that Redl lived an extravagant lifestyle, well beyond the means of a military officer's salary, owning several luxury apartments and sports cars. Redl accumulated thousands of crowns in debt, so perhaps money was sufficient motivation.

Redl managed to hide his duplicity in plain sight for some time. When suspicions arose, he framed operatives under his control and delivered them for prosecution. As the nations of Europe stumbled toward the cataclysm of WWI, it's believed he gave the Russians details of the Austro-Hungarian plans in the event of war, their offensive strategy against Serbia (Russia's ally and the likely target of Austro-Hungarian arms), and even the blueprints of border fortifications intended to protect his nation's frontier.

Redl conducted his profitable but despicable enterprise through the spring of 1913. He had stepped down from the Evidenzbureau the prior year and become chief of staff of the army's VIII Corps. As his clandestine activities continued, so too did the cash payments. But eventually the spymaster's surprising sloppiness, paired with the diligence of Major Maximilian Ronge, his protégé and successor as head of counterintelligence, proved Redl's undoing.

The practice of reading mail had become standard under Ronge, and one strange general delivery letter addressed to Nikon Nizetas was intercepted and found to contain only a large sum of cash. Suspicious, Ronge ordered that another envelope should be mailed to the same individual. When the recipient came to the local post office to claim it the source of a suspected intelligence leak would be revealed.

The follow-up letter was mailed on 9 May 1913, and when it was finally picked up two weeks later Ronge's agents trailed their suspect only to lose him after he hailed a taxi. Minutes later, the taxi driver returned to his station. Ronge's agents persuaded the driver to take them to the location where his earlier fare had exited, Vienna's Hotel Klomser, where Redl was a guest. Redl was confronted and confessed.

Army officers provided the traitor with a pistol, allowing him to commit suicide – most likely to avoid humiliation for the colossal breach of security that would become painfully evident during a trial. Redl obliged on 25 May 1913, after scrawling a final note that read: "Passion and levity have destroyed me. I pay with my life for my sins. Pray for me."

The saga of Redl and his espionage continues to fascinate. He has been the subject of historic investigation for over a century, with filmmakers, authors, and sleuths still searching for answers regarding Redl's motivation and the extent of the damage his treachery caused.

ABOVE For more than a decade, Alfred Redl sold state secrets to Imperial Russia

SELLER OF STATE SECRETS

BENEDICT ARNOLD

AMERICA'S FALLEN PATRIOT

Benedict Arnold epitomises treason for Americans, but without him the American Revolution might have failed

WORDS | MARC DESANTIS

In the United States, Benedict Arnold ranks as the worst of traitors. His very name is a byword for treachery. But without his efforts during the early years of the War of Independence, the American colonies' bid for freedom from Great Britain would likely have failed.

When war broke out in 1775, Arnold, then a Connecticut merchant, quickly joined the Patriot cause (Patriots wanted independence from Britain). He helped seize Fort Ticonderoga on Lake Champlain and its enormous stock of artillery pieces. Colonel Arnold's valour during the failed Patriot invasion of Canada in 1775–76 was outstanding – he suffered a musket ball wound in his left leg during a New Year's Eve attack on Quebec amidst a dreadful blizzard. Promoted afterward to brigadier general in the Continental Army, Arnold was the epitome of the physically courageous commander.

Arnold would spend much time operating in the strategically located colony of New York. If the Hudson River valley fell under British control, the links between the New England colonies and the others would be severed. In October 1776, though Arnold lost the naval Battle of Valcour Island, on Lake Champlain, it was not an unmitigated disaster. Because he had constructed several vessels on the lake, the British, under the command of General Guy Carleton, had to spend precious time building ships of their own to deal with him. This delayed the British southward movement to gain access to the northern Hudson River, and so their bid to divide and conquer the American colonies in 1776 failed, with Carleton subsequently going into winter quarters. Arnold had done his country an immense service. It would not be his last.

PROMOTIONS AND ALLEGATIONS

Though Arnold was rightfully first in line for a promotion to major general, on 19 February 1777, five other brigadier generals were boosted above him to that coveted rank. No good military reason could be made for these preferments. Instead, it was politically motivated, done as part of an ongoing conflict between the Continental Congress and the Continental Army.

Arnold saw this as a gross insult to him, and he was extremely prickly about his personal honour. It should be remembered that an 18th-century gentleman's honour was of tremendous importance, and what today may be considered a slight of minimal consequence could back then have been quite the opposite. Arnold was left a disgruntled senior officer with no recourse since Congress did not need to account for its decision-making.

Further, Arnold's contributions to the Patriot cause did not win him admiration in all American circles. The indisputably brave Arnold was abrasive and had a habit of finding himself at odds with other American officers. He was not always in the wrong, but he made himself many enemies. A long-standing grievance exploited by such men against Arnold concerned the accounting for the funds he expended during the abortive Canadian invasion. In May 1777, Arnold made his case directly to the Continental Congress in Philadelphia. He insisted that he had paid for what supplies he needed but unfortunately, in the catastrophe that befell the Americans, he had lost so many records that he could scarcely prove having spent more than a fraction of the money that Congress had appropriated.

Congress decided that Arnold was not at fault, but he was again snubbed for a promotion, and his seniority

BENEDICT ARNOLD

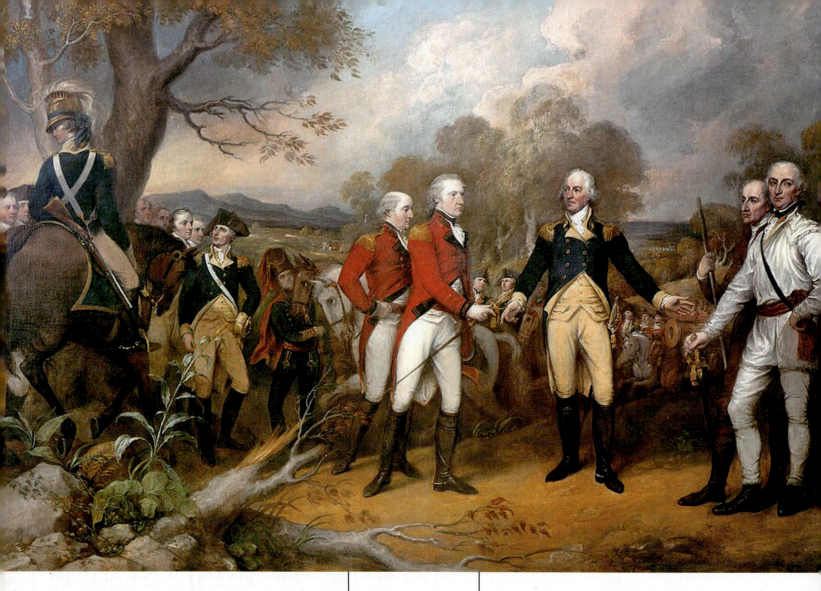

would not be restored until November. He resigned his commission that July. "Honour is a sacrifice no man ought to make," he wrote in his resignation letter.

HERO OF SARATOGA

Despite his resignation, Arnold was once more in the field in New York in late summer 1777. A large force of British soldiers under General John Burgoyne descended from Canada to try once again to detach New England from the other colonies. In September, his army reached the vicinity of a town named Saratoga on the Hudson River. On 19 September, at the Battle of Freeman's Farm, Arnold acted boldly to get his Continental Army troops into action before Burgoyne could bring his cannon into position to shoot at the Patriot defence works. His move also prevented the British from outflanking the Americans. Though the outcome of the fight favoured the British, because they had stood their ground while the Continentals backed off, it had been costly, and Burgoyne recognised Arnold's crucial role, noting his "perseverance in the attack on [Burgoyne's] lines".

In October, the two armies were still encamped near Saratoga. The Americans, under the overall command of Major General Horatio Gates, held a strong position. On 7 October, in the Battle of Bemis Heights, Arnold galloped across the field, again showing extraordinary physical courage. He was "more

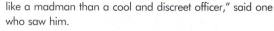

ABOVE The American victories at Saratoga, in which Benedict Arnold played important roles, ushered in French support for the Revolution

BELOW British Army Major John André was hanged by George Washington for plotting to seize West Point

like a madman than a cool and discreet officer," said one who saw him.

Arnold also astutely recognised the importance of a British officer who was maintaining the enemy's right wing. Arnold called for a marksman, and the enemy general, Simon Fraser, was soon downed. The British line began to unravel. With night coming on, Arnold attacked Breymann's Redoubt, a fortification held mostly by German soldiers in British service. The Redoubt succumbed to Continental assault, but not before Arnold had taken a musket ball in his left leg, the same limb that had been hit while on campaign in Canada.

Burgoyne would surrender his army less than two weeks later. The American victory at the Battles of Saratoga, in which Arnold had played such large parts, helped convince France that the Colonials had a chance of victory, and eventually an alliance emerged between the United States and France. Tangible benefits would include French financial support and eventually French troops in North America. Saratoga was the turning point in the American War of Independence, and without Arnold's contribution there, victory might have remained out of reach.

THE WEST POINT PLOT

Arnold was rankled that the commander-in-chief at Saratoga, Gates, who had taken no direct part in the fighting, was made out to be the great hero, while he himself was merely given

BENEDICT ARNOLD

the 'thanks of Congress'. Arnold's seniority in rank was not even immediately restored, as he might well have expected. It was all dirty, corrupt politics to Arnold, who felt underappreciated. And despite the inception of the French alliance, the years following Saratoga were tough ones for the Patriot cause, and it seemed to many that the American Revolution would collapse. Arnold was one of those who started to lose faith.

In April 1779, Arnold married his second wife, Peggy Shippen, whose Philadelphia family was thought to be Loyalist (pro-British) in outlook. In May of that same year, he made overtures to British General Sir Henry Clinton. A treasonous pact was made, but Arnold would bide his time until he could be of most use to the Crown. Outwardly, he was still a Patriot.

General George Washington, commander-in-chief of the Continental Army, valued Arnold's generalship. With no inkling that Arnold was now in league with the British, he gave Arnold the command of the Hudson Highland army, which Arnold assumed in August 1780. Washington had in fact first offered him a field command, something more befitting Arnold's amply demonstrated battlefield talents.

Arnold cited his crippling injury as the reason for turning down the field command, but he had purposefully sought control of the crucial fort of West Point on the Hudson River: as part of his pact with Clinton he was to hand it over to the British. His 'fee' would be £20,000, roughly equal to several million U.S. dollars today. It was a substantial sum, but cheap for the British if it brought an end to the war, because West Point prevented the Royal Navy from moving along the Hudson River. The colonies would be easily split thereafter.

But the plot was discovered by chance. Washington himself was to meet with Arnold at his West Point headquarters in late September 1780. Major John André of the British Army in the meanwhile had been arrested by Patriot militia on 23 September while carrying incriminating papers concerning the handover. Arnold, getting word of André's apprehension, escaped from his post not long before Washington arrived there on the 25th. Arnold found refuge aboard *HMS* Vulture, and spent the rest of the war fighting against his former comrades-in-arms.

Washington was furious. "Arnold has betrayed us," he fumed. "Whom can we trust now?" Washington sought to trade André for Arnold, but Clinton refused and the major was hanged for spying.

Arnold's countrymen were left stunned, but not silent. "Treason of the blackest dye was yesterday discovered," stated the orderly book of one Samuel Frost of the Continental Army, concerning Arnold's plot. Within days, word of Arnold's infamy had spread to Philadelphia and Patriots were burning him in effigy. "Never since the fall of Lucifer," said Patriot General Nathanael Greene, "has a fall equalled his."

To make full sense of Colonial Arnold's treason is difficult. He was so often dwelling on what he saw as slights and injustices, of which to his mind there had been many, in addition to the allegations about his handling of money during the Canadian campaign. He saw his countrymen as being venal and ingrates, and his belief in the Revolution curdled. Yet was all that enough to change sides, especially when such trust had been placed in him by none other than George Washington himself?

Arnold would die in London in June 1801 at the age of 60. Though his memory in his homeland is forever associated with treason, his valour is still recalled. A monument in the shape of Arnold's left boot stands in Saratoga in honour of his courage in attacking Breymann's Redoubt. Erected in 1887, it commemorates the "most brilliant soldier of the Continental Army", but Arnold's name appears nowhere on it.

TOP Arnold's action at the Battle of Valcour Bay on Lake Champlain in 1776 delayed the British advance, preventing them from dividing the American colonies

ABOVE Though General Guy Carleton was victorious at the Battle of Valcour Bay, Arnold's stiff resistance stymied the British 1776 offensive

"TREASON OF THE BLACKEST DYE WAS YESTERDAY DISCOVERED"

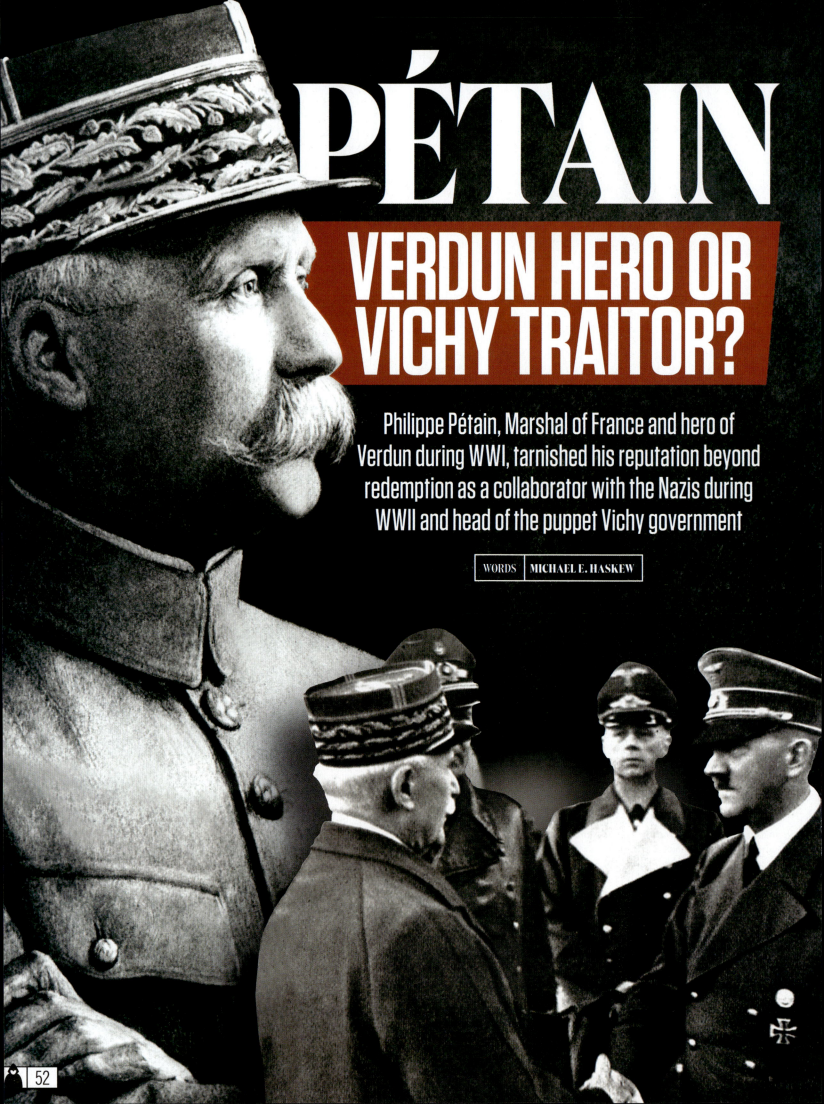

PÉTAIN

VERDUN HERO OR VICHY TRAITOR?

Philippe Pétain, Marshal of France and hero of Verdun during WWI, tarnished his reputation beyond redemption as a collaborator with the Nazis during WWII and head of the puppet Vichy government

WORDS | MICHAEL E. HASKEW

PÉTAIN

Marshal Henri Philippe Pétain was a prominent figure in French political and military affairs during the first half of the 20th century. One of the most enigmatic individuals of modern history, Pétain became a national hero during the epic struggle at Verdun in World War I but tarnished his reputation beyond redemption a generation later by collaborating with the Nazis in 1940 and serving as head of the puppet Vichy government during World War II.

Pétain was an officer of the French Army, military strategist and tactician, diplomat and politician. His career with the French Army spanned 46 years, during which he served as commander of all French troops during World War I, chief of staff of the army and minister of war. He also served as deputy prime minister and prime minister of the French Republic during the dark early days of World War II. Pétain subsequently became chief of the French State of Vichy, the puppet regime subservient to Adolf Hitler and the Nazis after the fall of France in the summer of 1940.

Pétain was born on 24 April 1856 in the village of Cauchy-á-la-Tour, in the Pas-de-Calais department of northern France. He was the son of a farmer, Omer-Venant, and his great uncle, Father Abbe Lefebvre, was a Catholic priest who had served in Napoleon's army. Tales of his great uncle's adventures during the fabled campaigns of that era convinced Philippe to pursue a military career.

Pétain was, for many years, a confirmed bachelor and womaniser. He did not marry until the autumn of 1920. His wife, Eugénie Hardon, was 43 years old and he was 64. The couple had no children. "Pétain was known as quick-witted and considered himself something of a ladies' man," says Dr. Jonathan Krause, lecturer in Modern European History at Hertford College, University of Oxford. "He first met his future wife during the pre-World War I period, and she was about six years old at the time. He was pursuing the mother and kept in touch with the daughter over the years."

MARCH TO THE MILITARY

In 1876, at the age of 20, Pétain enlisted in the French Army. He graduated from the prestigious French Military Academy at St Cyr near the bottom of his class, 403rd of 412. Although his academic career was undistinguished, he managed to gain an assignment to the Chasseurs à pied, the army's elite light infantry unit. Pétain also attended the École Supérieure de Guerre, the Army War College, in Paris, but his performance there too was unremarkable.

"During the period of the 1880s there weren't a lot of opportunities for advancement," says Krause. "Pétain was never at the top of his class at any stage of his education but, interestingly, he did find himself in an elite infantry unit. He was always fairly political and tried to put himself in position for political power, but he was a prickly character and known as deeply sarcastic, so he was not able to win many friends."

By 1890, Pétain had been promoted to the rank of captain and assigned to the 15th Corps. Two years later he was elevated to command the 3rd Battalion of Chasseurs, headquartered at Vincennes. For the next decade Pétain held assignments as a staff officer to the military commander of Paris and trained in artillery and ordnance, becoming an authority on the topics.

Pétain favoured concentrated firepower, delivered by heavy guns, over the massed infantry attack that was intended to decide an engagement at the point of the bayonet or the obsolescent cavalry charge. His views were somewhat controversial but their veracity was borne out on the battlefields of World War I as outmoded tactics cost the lives of many thousands of soldiers, failing in the face of new technology, particularly the lethal machine gun that swept the open ground of no-man's land between the opposing trenches.

INTO THE GREAT WAR

Pétain's controversial views on the conduct of modern warfare undoubtedly impacted his upward mobility in the French Army prior to World War I. On the eve of the conflict he was a rather obscure 58-year-old colonel commanding an infantry brigade, but as the war progressed his theories of concentrated firepower gained momentum and promotion came steadily. Advancement was partially due to the sobering fact that many French officers had been killed in action seeking glory on the battlefield while leading their troops in suicidal frontal attacks against German machine guns and paying with their lives.

By now a colonel, Pétain led his brigade into action at the Battle of Guise in late August 1914. The result was a thorough defeat for the French, and Pétain was promoted to brigadier general a day after the fighting subsided. He replaced General Pierre Peslin, who committed suicide in despair. Swiftly, Pétain was given command of the 6th Infantry Division and took part in the First Battle of the Marne. He was promoted again in October and took command of the XXXIII Corps, participating in the Artois

OPPOSITE, BOTTOM Marshal Pétain shakes hands with Adolf Hitler at Montoire on 24 October 1940 in a deal that established the puppet state of Vichy
BELOW General Pétain decorates two flags with the Legion of Honour, France, 1917

"PÉTAIN FAVOURED CONCENTRATED FIREPOWER, DELIVERED BY HEAVY GUNS, OVER THE MASSED INFANTRY ATTACK THAT WAS INTENDED TO DECIDE AN ENGAGEMENT AT THE POINT OF THE BAYONET"

Offensive in the spring of 1915. By mid-summer he was leading the entire 2nd Army.

CRUCIBLE OF VERDUN

In the winter of 1916, the French Army was embroiled in a deadly struggle with the Germans at Verdun, a fortified city on the River Meuse, 200 kilometres (124 miles) east of Paris. The Germans, led by General Erich von Falkenhayn and Crown Prince Wilhelm, eldest son of Kaiser Wilhelm II, had launched the major operation with the intent to bleed the French forces white, inflicting so many casualties that France might be compelled to seek an armistice due to lack of manpower available to prosecute the war (France would ultimately lose 163,000 dead in the battle).

The French, under Field Marshal Joseph Joffre, were preoccupied with events elsewhere and slow to respond to the German buildup of forces in the vicinity of Verdun. When they did respond the French committed tremendous resources to hold the fortified city and a gruesome battle of attrition ensued.

The Battle of Verdun began on 21 February 1916, and the Germans made significant advances during the opening phase. When the 2nd Army was ordered into action, General Pétain became conspicuous among the troops, frequently visiting his men on the front lines while few other officers dared venture close to the fighting. In doing so Pétain bolstered the morale of his men and in turn they greatly admired him. On 25 February, he was elevated to command all French forces in the Région Fortifiée de Verdun, and in May he was promoted to command of Army Group Centre. As an artilleryman the general recognised the inherent inefficiency of the French heavy guns. He brought in additional heavy-calibre weapons and reoriented their focus to achieve better results, particularly against the German flanks. He was known to personally evaluate and adjust firing coordinates of individual guns, improving accuracy along with the efficient use of scarce ammunition.

"Obviously, Verdun began poorly for the French," observes Krause. "They were outnumbered and outgunned, and the Germans had taken up excellent positions

> **CLOCKWISE FROM TOP LEFT** Petain, pictured here c.1916; Pétain talks to King George V, 12 July 1917; Pétain pictured in his private railway carriage at Verdun, August 1916; This Vichy government propaganda poster depicts Pétain above members of the youth organisation Compagnons de France; A Vichy-era badge bearing the regime's motto of "Work, Family, Homeland"

Pétain pictured in uniform During World War I he was made Marshal of France

"GENERAL PÉTAIN BECAME CONSPICUOUS AMONG THE TROOPS, FREQUENTLY VISITING HIS MEN ON THE FRONT LINES WHILE FEW OTHER OFFICERS DARED VENTURE CLOSE TO THE FIGHTING"

A military parade beneath a banner depicting Vichy head of state Pétain

surrounding them. When Pétain took command he took care of some long-standing issues with the troops. He increased things like leave and introduced more rapid rotation of troops from the front line to keep troops healthy and at their fighting best, while the Germans left people in the lines for long periods and their combat efficiency would diminish."

At the age of 60, Pétain exuded vitality. He praised the brave and cashiered 'cowards' from the combat zone, and his rotation policy – known as *noria* – helped preserve the combat capability of beleaguered French soldiers. The French continually wrestled with supply deficiencies, depending on a single narrow road that was nicknamed the Vioe Sacrée, or Sacred Way. Pétain ensured that this supply line remained open and improved a light railway into the French defensive salient to enhance logistics.

French forces at Verdun eventually grew to more than a million soldiers, and Pétain's grasp of the situation saved the Allied cause from a catastrophic defeat. The motto "On ne passé pas!", or "They shall not pass!", became a rallying cry. By early summer the critical moment at Verdun had passed. The fighting continued until mid-December, and the French line held.

> "AT THE AGE OF 60, PÉTAIN EXUDED VITALITY. HE PRAISED THE BRAVE AND CASHIERED 'COWARDS' FROM THE COMBAT ZONE"

ABOVE By now a national hero, Pétain talks to his staff at his headquarters, 1918

BELOW The Vichy leader is greeted by adoring crowds, 30 July 1944

NATIONAL HERO

After his performance at Verdun, Pétain was lauded as a national hero and named commander-in-chief of the army in the spring of 1917. He ruthlessly quelled a mutiny within the ranks and for the remainder of the Great War maintained a command role subordinate only to General Ferdinand Foch, who was chief of the general staff and supreme commander of Allied forces. Pétain was elevated to the rank of Marshal of France on 21 November 1918, just ten days after the armistice.

Throughout the inter-war period he was the best-known soldier of France. "Pétain's military career pretty well ends following World War I," says Krause, "but he is a celebrity in Paris and lives the life of someone who is perceived as one of the saviours of France, yet he isn't someone that you would necessarily imagine being a person of great political influence 20 years later."

Nevertheless, Pétain did exert some influence on the French political scene and the military preparations to perhaps fight another major war in Europe. He contributed to the design and location of tactical strongpoints along the Maginot Line, a string of fortifications intended to dissuade the Germans from invading France from the east, and he served briefly as minister of war in the 1930s during a period of austerity in defence spending due to the huge cost of the Great War and impact of the Great Depression. There was talk of his rising to head of state, and in 1939 he was appointed ambassador to Spain.

TWILIGHT OF COLLABORATION

Even as the aged Marshal Pétain assumed his diplomatic role, war clouds gathered over Europe once more. The rise of Nazi Germany threatened the peace, and the storm broke on 1 September 1939 with Adolf Hitler's invasion of Poland. Both France and Great Britain, obligated by treaty to come to the aid of Poland, declared war on Germany.

The early months of World War II in the west of Europe were rather uneventful. During a period derisively called the Sitzkrieg, or Phoney War, the lines were static. Allied and German troops eyed one another warily but refrained from sustained combat. Then, on 10 May 1940, the Germans launched Fall Gelb, or Case Yellow, their invasion of France and the Low Countries.

After the war Pétain claimed he had cooperated with Hitler to protect the French from further Nazi excesses
LEFT Hermann Göring meets Pétain in Saint-Florentin, December 1941

The tremendous German onslaught drove the French and British back, and Prime Minister Paul Reynaud resigned on 17 June 1940, three days after Paris fell to the advancing enemy. The 84-year-old Marshal Pétain was appointed as Reynaud's successor. As France reeled from its sudden and total defeat Pétain led a defeatist faction of the government, advocating an armistice with the Germans rather than continuing a fight that he considered hopeless. He offered the French people the "gift of his person" and promised to remain in France rather than attempting to flee to the colonies of North Africa or the safety of Britain as other military and political leaders had.

With the honour of France in tatters, Pétain met with Hitler just eight days after the Nazis paraded through the streets of the French capital and negotiated a debilitating peace agreement that established the puppet state of Vichy. The humiliation of France was complete as Pétain accepted the post of Vichy head of state. He openly collaborated with the Nazis, exerting authoritarian control, sanctioning the repression of French Jewry and enacting right-wing laws. He gave the Nazis free rein to round up non-French Jews and deport them to concentration camps in Germany and the occupied territories.

"The standard explanation, the usual sort of line, is that Pétain was so scared by the losses in World War I that he was not willing to suffer that again," says Krause. "His conservatism and, I believe probably his anti-Semitism, effectively gave him the reasoning to relinquish control of France to Nazi Germany."

Pétain placed a death sentence in absentia on Free French leader Charles de Gaulle, his one-time protégé, and brought his own deputy, the odious Pierre Laval, a man who sent thousands of his countryman into slavery in occupied Poland and Nazi Germany, to the forefront of Vichy diplomacy in the spring of 1942. The pro-Nazi government offered the people of France a "national revival", displacing the well-known slogan of the French Republic – "Liberte, Equality, Fraternity" – with a sombre and hollow "Work, Family, Homeland."

"I don't see how anyone could say that Pétain was not complicit with the Nazis in many ways, including the deportation of Jews to Nazi Germany," says Krause. "His

> "HIS ICONIC REPUTATION FROM WORLD WAR I WAS NOT NEARLY ENOUGH TO COUNTER HIS COLLABORATION WITH THE NAZIS. ONCE YOU CROSS SUCH A LINE, THERE JUST ISN'T MUCH THAT CAN BE DONE ABOUT IT"

iconic reputation from World War I was not nearly enough to counter his collaboration with the Nazis. Once you cross such a line, there just isn't much that can be done about it."

Retribution for Pétain and the Vichy collaborationists came swiftly after the Allied victory in World War II. Laval was tried, convicted of treason and executed on 15 October 1945. Pétain was also put on trial, wearing the uniform of a Marshal of France throughout the proceedings. He asserted that he was not answerable to the tribunal and said, "The High Court, as constituted, does not represent the French people, and it is to them alone that the Marshal of France, Head of State, will address himself."

Pétain claimed that he had played a "double game", collaborating with the Nazis while attempting to safeguard his people from further excesses during the occupation. He was quiet for the remainder of the trial, and the extent of his cooperation with the Nazis was readily apparent. He was convicted of treason in the summer of 1945 and sentenced to death. However, in an act of mercy to a man who would have seen him dead, de Gaulle stepped in and commuted the sentence to life in prison on the grounds of Pétain's age. With the exception of the rank of Marshal of France, Pétain was stripped of all military honours and titles.

"Pétain is still a low figure in French history, a bête noir, if you will, and for good reason" Krause concludes. "He was prominent during one of the darkest periods in the history of France, so France has had to be conscious of its image during World War II, not just its defeat in 1940 but what is properly shameful in the amount of collaboration with the Nazis that took place across French society. Then there is the talk that the size and importance of the French resistance to the Nazis is actually exaggerated. It puts France as a nation on the right side of history, but it is an impossible position."

Certainly, Pétain is remembered as being on the wrong side. He was exiled to the windswept Ile d'Yeu south of the Brittany peninsula to live out his life in ignominy. And a long life it was. He died on the desolate island on 23 July 1951 at the age of 95 and was buried there. Perhaps fittingly, his last wish to be interred among the soldiers who had fallen under his command at Verdun was denied by the government of France. He remains a widely despised figure in his homeland to this day.

PÉTAIN

Pétain wore his military uniform throughout his trial for treason

TEN TRAGIC DAYS

La Decena Trágica (the Ten Tragic Days) plunged Mexico into a bloody standoff that saw General Victoriano Huerta snatch power from the president and in turn become his country's biggest traitor

WORDS | EDOARDO ALBERT

It was an ordinary house. Nothing remarkable about it. Just another house in the Roma district of Mexico City. But as General Victoriano Huerta stood outside the door, waiting for his knock to be answered, he knew that entering the house was to step across the threshold into a different life. For it was within those walls that he proposed to bring down the duly elected president of Mexico and become president himself. Huerta had sent discreet messages to the man waiting to meet him inside, hinting at what he proposed, but he had carefully left out any suggestion that he expected the top job to come to him. General Félix Díaz, the man he was about to meet, expected that he himself would become president. Huerta shook his head; Díaz had neither the brains nor the ruthlessness required to take the opportunity in front of them. But he had.

The opportunity had arrived just two days earlier, on 9 February 1913. Two years previously, in October 1911, Mexico had elected Francisco Madero president in a landslide vote. Madero took power after decades of increasingly authoritarian rule by Porfirio Díaz (if that surname looks familiar, it's because Porfirio Díaz was the uncle of General Félix Díaz). President Díaz had been driven from power following a popular uprising, and the new President Madero's government was greeted with great hope, and even greater expectations, by the people who had elected him.

Unfortunately, Madero had been unable to meet all those hopes and dreams of change turned into bitter disappointment. Radicals thought his reforms too timid, whereas supporters of the old regime resented the changes Madero attempted to bring in. By the end of 1912, Madero found himself facing revolts around the country, led by both radicals and conservatives. Madero had no choice but to face the uprisings. The general who proved most ruthlessly efficient at doing this was Victoriano Huerta, a soldier of the old regime but one who had apparently proved his loyalty to Madero by crushing the rebels.

Then, on 9 February 1913, the rebels appeared in the political and population centre of Mexico: Mexico City. Soldiers attacked two prisons, freeing generals Félix Díaz and Bernardo Reyes, who had been imprisoned following their previous attempts to overthrow the government. General Reyes immediately led an attack on the city's Presidential Palace but was shot and killed.

President Madero was not at the palace when it was attacked. When news reached him of the attempted coup, he rode back into the city. Reaching his destination, Madero stopped near the National Theatre to gather intelligence about the situation, and while he made phone calls and sent out messengers, various officials arrived to take orders from their president.

Among these was Victoriano Huerta. Health problems had forced Huerta to step back from military duties, but now he offered to command the president's forces as they responded to the attempted coup. Madero had passed over Huerta when appointing his minister of war, to the general's obvious resentment. But Madero knew Huerta to be

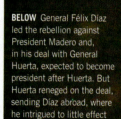

BELOW General Félix Díaz led the rebellion against President Madero and, in his deal with General Huerta, expected to become president after Huerta. But Huerta reneged on the deal, sending Díaz abroad, where he intrigued to little effect

TEN TRAGIC DAYS

a brutally efficient officer, and he was now offering to help. Madero placed Huerta in charge of the army. It would prove a fatal decision.

Although the attack on the Presidential Palace had failed, General Díaz led the remaining rebels to the city armoury, the Ciudadela. This was a formidable fort, and, being the main arsenal for the city garrison, it was well-stocked with weapons and artillery. From the arsenal, the rebels began firing cannons at the Presidential Palace. For the next two days, the presidential and rebel forces exchanged artillery fire from their respective redoubts in the Presidential Palace and the Ciudadela. Many civilians were caught in the crossfire, but little changed militarily.

Then, on 11 February, General Huerta met General Díaz secretly. Later that day, Huerta ordered the finest government troops into a very open position in what proved to be a doomed attack on the Ciudadela. Many of the best troops loyal to Madero's government were killed.

For the next four days, the bombardments continued, killing hundreds of civilians. Political support for Madero's government began to fracture at its failure to suppress the revolt. The U.S. ambassador, Henry Lane Wilson, who despised Madero, began to marshal support for his removal, leading to increasing pressure on the president to resign. Finally, on the evening of 15 February, Wilson brokered a ceasefire for the following day, a Sunday, so that the dead could be recovered and decently buried. But while wheelbarrows carted the dead from the streets, messengers scurried between General Huerta, Ambassador Wilson and General Díaz.

> **"MADERO PLACED HUERTA IN CHARGE OF THE ARMY. IT WOULD PROVE A FATAL DECISION"**

BELOW Victoriano Huerta, Mexico's greatest traitor, was himself everything that the man he betrayed was trying to promote

Now, for the first time, Huerta declared his hand to people outside the immediate band of rebels, receiving assurance of U.S. support in return.

During the next day, Monday, 17 February, Huerta carefully laid out his plans, ensuring that he had the support of the military under his command. With the support of the men with guns, he was ready to act. On Tuesday, 18 February, Huerta's men arrested Madero's brother, Gustavo, and then the president himself. At 9 p.m., Victoriano Huerta arrived at the U.S. embassy for a conference with General Díaz, under the auspices of Ambassador Wilson, to determine who would take control of Mexico. Although Díaz wanted the presidency and attempted to argue it was his by right of successful rebellion, Huerta had the men and the now-arrested president. It was an impasse.

General Huerta, however, was the far more formidable and ruthless personality at the meeting. After three hours in the smoking room, the men emerged with their pact signed. According to the deal, Huerta would become provisional president but hold elections later in the year for which he would stand down in favour of Díaz. It was a deal Huerta signed with as much faith as his promise to put down the rebellion against President Madero. With the agreement signed, the president's brother was handed over to Díaz's supporters and murdered.

On 18 February, Huerta telegrammed U.S. President William Taft: "I have the honor to inform you that I have overthrown this Government. The armed forces support me, and from now on peace and prosperity will reign."

To give the coup some semblance of legitimacy, Madero and the vice president, Pino Suárez, who had

TEN TRAGIC DAYS

LEFT The fighting in Mexico City was brutal but haphazard – particularly as Huerta deliberately prevented his men from putting down the rebellion

also been arrested, were pressured into resigning their offices. The previous president, Porfirio Díaz, had been allowed to go into exile after he resigned, so they had every reason to expect similar treatment. However, Huerta would prove more ruthless than they had imagined.

But while merciless, Huerta was also a stickler for constitutional protocols. With both president and vice president having resigned, that left the foreign minister as the man in charge. Seeing the writing on the wall, the foreign minister took charge of Mexico for 45 minutes on Thursday, 20 February, long enough for him to appoint General Huerta as the minister of the interior before he resigned in turn. Thus, according to the Mexican constitution, Victoriano Huerta, the new minister of the interior and the next highest official in the land, became president of the republic. All nice and legal.

However, this still left the question of what to do with Madero and Suárez. It did not take long for Mexico to find out the answer.

At 11:45 a.m. on 22 February, the two men were driven from the Presidential Palace towards a nearby prison, but rather than drive into the prison, the line of cars swung round it, stopping in the open ground behind it. A group of reporters waiting at the prison chased after the cars, only to hear a volley of shots. When they reached the scene they found Madero and Suárez lying dead on the ground. Major Francisco Cárdenas, the commanding officer of the soldiers who had escorted them, claimed that the two men had died in a crossfire as another group of men attempted to rescue them. Of the supposed rescuers there was no sign. Madero, dead at 39, was buried in the capital's French cemetery.

Huerta never admitted to ordering the murder of Madero and Suárez, but their deaths turned them both – particularly Madero – into martyrs. As president, Francisco Madero had struggled with the hopes placed upon him, but as a martyr he became the emblem of the forces that arrayed themselves against Victoriano Huerta's regime. Such was Madero's potency in death that, despite his ruthlessness, Huerta only remained president from 22 February 1913 to 15 July 1914. In the face of the opposition that threatened to overwhelm him, Huerta resigned – but in his case he survived, going into exile in Spain.

Huerta attempted to make a political comeback in 1915, arriving in the United States and travelling down to the border with Mexico, but he was arrested by U.S. officials and died in custody, probably from cirrhosis of the liver brought on by heavy drinking.

The tragic irony of Victoriano Huerta's life is that he is remembered as the great traitor of Mexican history, the man who betrayed a reformist president in Francisco Madero who had come to power promising to raise up the poor and oppressed of Mexico. But Madero was himself the child of one of the richest families in Mexico and came from European stock, whereas Huerta was born dirt-poor and his parents were both said to be Huichol; Huerta never pretended to be anything other than of indigenous heritage. Indeed, he entered the military in order to escape the poverty of his upbringing.

So the poor child of indigenous parents brought down the rich, white Madero – the man who had come to power by promising to support people like Huerta. It would be almost comical if it weren't so tragic.

63

RIGHT Varus, depicted here by Italian actor Gaetano Aronica in the Netflix series *Barbarians*

THE BETRAYAL OF ROME

How a Roman citizen lured three of the empire's legions into a deadly trap

WORDS | EDOARDO ALBERT

THE BETRAYAL OF ROME

It was over. As Publius Quinctilius Varus, commander of the XVII, XVIII and XIX legions, looked at the carnage surrounding him, he knew all hope was lost. For three days they had tried to fight their way to safety, through appalling conditions of mud and rain, while the Germans harassed and assaulted his retreating legions. The commander of the cavalry, Numonius Vala, had abandoned them with the surviving horsemen, trying to ride to safety. Now the native barbarians were amassing for the final assault on the remnants still under Varus' command. He knew what the Germans did with men they captured in battle. But it was the disgrace that was worse. His name forever tainted. As the screams and battle cries drew closer, the general fixed his sword point up in the muddy earth and fell upon it.

When the battle was over, the Germans found Varus' body, impaled by his own sword. The man who had masterminded the plan that had seen the almost total destruction of three Roman legions, Arminius, commanded that Varus' head be cut off and sent as a gift to the leader of the only important German tribal federation not to have taken part in the battle. The head was a message of what Arminius had achieved and a promise of what they could do as allies. Its refusal marked the limits of Arminius' extraordinary victory among his German rivals. But for the Romans it would outline the limits of an empire that they had previously believed would expand forever.

It was not supposed to be like this. Under Augustus, the Roman state had enjoyed a period of unprecedented internal peace after a century of civil wars while also expanding its frontiers in all directions. Between 12 and 9 BCE, Augustus' adopted son, Drusus, had pushed into Germania, conquering swathes of territory and subjecting German tribes to Roman rule. Roman expansion continued under Tiberius (the brother of Drusus, who had died in 9 CE), but before he could complete the conquest Tiberius was forced to march south to deal with a revolt in the Balkans. The revolt lasted for four years, and it would require the efforts of all the eight legions Tiberius took with him to finally extinguish it.

In his absence, Augustus appointed Varus, an experienced, not to say brutal, administrator as governor of the new imperial province of Germania. To understand the inner workings of the German tribes across the River Rhine, Varus turned to a man who knew them better than any other: a young Roman citizen of the rank of equites (just below the senatorial class) named Arminius. It was to prove a fatal mistake.

For Arminius was German and, under his Roman veneer, he had resolved to stop the Romans conquering Germania. Arminius was his Latin name. His original German name was not recorded for it was not needed when the young Arminius came to Rome as a hostage to guarantee the good behaviour of his kinsmen. In Rome, Arminius learned Latin and served in the Roman army with sufficient distinction to be made a citizen and to be raised to the rank of equites. His Roman military service gave Arminius a thorough understanding of Roman tactics and formations, a knowledge he would put to devastating use when he returned to his native Germania.

His subsequent deeds indicate that Arminius must have been a highly effective commander. He was given charge of a unit of auxiliaries, and when his unit was transferred to Germania he quickly became one of Varus' most trusted advisers. While ingratiating himself with Varus, Arminius simultaneously made contact with the Germanic tribes across the Rhine. He himself was a member of the Cherusci tribe who lived in the region of present-day Hanover, and Varus often employed him as a messenger to the hostile tribes. This gave Arminius the perfect opportunity to form and cement an alliance of the Germanic tribes while gathering intelligence of Roman intentions.

When Tiberius stripped eight legions from the German frontier to help put down the Great Illyrian Revolt in the Balkans, Arminius saw that he had the perfect opportunity to strike at the Romans. As governor of Syria, Varus had earned a reputation for brutality, crucifying 2,000 Jewish rebels. Varus no doubt pursued the same harsh path in Germania, making it easier for Arminius to unite the usually warring and suspicious tribes under his secret leadership.

With the tribes onside, the final strand of Arminius' plan was to lure the Romans into a battle in a place of his own choosing. Having fought alongside the Romans many times, Arminius was well aware that in open ground the disciplined legions would cut down the waves of German warriors like a military threshing machine. To have any chance of victory he had to ensure the Romans were forced to fight in the sort of terrain that made it all but impossible for them to adopt their battlefield formations.

So when Arminius came to Varus with reports that the Bructeri tribe in northwest Germania had revolted, he had in mind exactly where he would bring the Romans to battle. Such was Varus' faith in his Latinised auxiliary commander that he ignored the warning of another German chief,

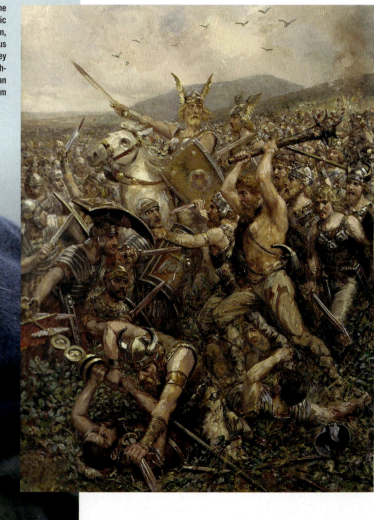

RIGHT Given the more Germanic name of Herman, Arminius became a key figure of 19th-century German nationalism

Segestes, that he was being led into a trap. Varus dismissed the warning as sour grapes on the part of Segestes, who did not approve of Arminius' relationship with his daughter Thusnelda, and set off into Germania to put down the Bructeri, taking the route that Arminius suggested.

While an experienced governor, Varus had less experience of military command. To ensure the success of his mission, he took all three legions under his command; the XVII, XVIII and XIX, some 20,000 legionaries, auxiliaries and associated camp followers.

It was early September but the weather was atrocious, with heavy rain soaking the marching army, turning the earth beneath their feet into a quagmire. At the end of the first day's march Arminius requested permission from Varus to summon German allies to join the expedition. Arminius had carefully seeded the belief in Varus that many of the German tribes were willing to fight alongside the Romans. Varus, his belief in Arminius' loyalty unshaken, gave him permission, and the German rode away with his men. Although he did not know it yet, Varus had sealed his fate and the fate of the men he was leading deep into the dense German forest.

As was their practice, the Roman forces threw up a camp in which to pass the night. Unknown to them, Arminius and his men were busy preparing the trap that they would march into on the morrow.

The path the Romans took the next day was narrow, threading through thick forest with a hill rising on one flank and a bog on the other. The legions had no choice but to spread out along the trail so that the column straggled through the forest. The line of Romans extended for at least 13 or 14 kilometres (eight or nine miles) through the trees. Unknown to Varus, Arminius had built fortifications along the hill beside which the Romans were marching. At his signal, the Germans launched their assault.

With the legions spread out, the ground wet and muddy, and Arminius probing at different points along the column throughout the day, Varus was unable to regroup his forces into any sort of fighting formation. Local struggles continued throughout the day. Whenever a group of legionaries attempted to launch a counterattack, the Germans retreated behind their fortifications.

Only nightfall brought an end to the carnage. The surviving legionaries erected a night camp behind fortifications while the Germans retired and waited for first light. Knowing their only salvation lay in making it back to Roman territory, Varus ordered a break out the next morning. The surviving legionaries managed to punch through the German blockade but at the cost of further casualties. With the Germans continuing to harry them, the Romans marched on, even attempting a night march in their efforts to escape the trap that Arminius had set. But their losses were mounting, and on the final day they entered the last killing zone that Arminius had prepared for them.

In the shadow of Kalkriese Hill, with an impassable bog preventing escape to the flank, the Romans found a trench cutting across their line of march and an earthwork flanking them from which the Germans continued to hurl missiles and spears. The Romans made a desperate attempt to storm the earthwork but were pushed back. Numonius Vala, the cavalry commander, attempted to escape with his surviving cavalrymen, but he was pursued and killed.

> "WHEN TIBERIUS STRIPPED EIGHT LEGIONS FROM THE GERMAN FRONTIER TO HELP PUT DOWN THE GREAT ILLYRIAN REVOLT IN THE BALKANS, ARMINIUS SAW THAT HE HAD THE PERFECT OPPORTUNITY TO STRIKE AT THE ROMANS"

BELOW A reproduction of the defensive wall that Arminius had built to protect his men and to stop the Romans escaping up the hill

THE BETRAYAL OF ROME

This was when Varus realised that all hope was gone. Rather than risk being taken captive he committed suicide. Many other officers did likewise. Abandoned by their commanders, the surviving legionaries fought on, but without direction they were surrounded and picked off. Of the 20,000 men that Varus took into the forest, only a handful escaped. The rest were killed, either during the battle or sacrificed to the tribal gods afterwards.

When news of the disaster reached Augustus in Rome, he was so upset that he hit his head against a wall, shouting, "Quintili Vare, legiones redde!" (Quintilius Varus, give me back my legions!).

It was a momentous victory. The empire that had no bounds now confronted a limit to its reach drawn in the blood of its soldiers: the Rhine would form its frontier for the rest of its existence. As for the man behind this stunning victory, Arminius would later marry Thusnelda against her father's wishes. Their union would produce a son, Thumelicus, who would grow up a prisoner of the Romans after he and his mother were later captured. Distraught at the loss of his wife and child, Arminius never wed again, and in 21 CE he was assassinated by political rivals.

The exact location of the battle remained disputed for centuries until 1987, when Major Tony Clunn, stationed in Osnabrück with the Royal Tank Regiment, decided to go searching with his metal detector. An amateur archaeologist, and through his military training well versed in spotting likely lines of march, Clunn set out to investigate the area under Kalkriese Hill. His metal detector soon started pinging. Digging beneath the soil, Major Clunn found a Roman denarius bearing the portrait of Augustus. He quickly found more coins, all dating from the reign of Augustus. Clunn marked the exact locations of his discoveries. There was only one likely reason for so many Augustan-era Roman coins to be scattered around on the slopes of Kalkriese Hill. Soon, professional archaeologists followed, undertaking systematic investigations that revealed the debris of battle along a 24-kilometre (15-mile) corridor running east to west.

Archaeological finds included traces of the wall that Arminius had built to contain and channel the Roman legions. Lots of debris was found in front of the wall, almost none behind it. The Romans had attempted to break through but been driven back, leaving traces of their doomed expedition in the ground for two millennia until the attention of Clunn brought them to the surface and allowed historians to trace the course of one of the most important battles in history through the landscape in which it occurred.

BELOW Some of the Roman coins that enabled archaeologists to chart the course of the ancient battle

BOTTOM RIGHT A rather fanciful portrait of Arminius: in reality, the real man escapes into the unknown, even his original name having been lost

BOTTOM LEFT A restorer works on a piece of Roman armour found during the excavations around Kalkriese Hill

MATA HARI

SPY OR SCAPEGOAT?

Discover the love, lies and tragic life of the accused exotic dancer who faced the firing squad

WORDS | GAVIN MORTIMER

Awoken in her Paris prison cell, Mata Hari pulled on her stockings, high-heeled slippers, long black velvet cloak and announced, "I am ready." She cut a striking figure, a woman who moved with the cool confidence of one accustomed to admiring glances. To a passerby she could have been on her way to just another performance, but this would be her last. Flanked by an army officer, her lawyer and two nuns, she was escorted to meet the firing squad.

It was not quite 6 a.m. when the car stopped and Mata stepped out, pulling her coat tight to keep out the chill autumnal air. She glanced at the 13 soldiers with what one eyewitness described as "disdain" and calmly walked towards a large wooden stake in front of a hummock of earth that would provide a backdrop for any stray bullets. When she was offered the customary blindfold, she asked, "Must I wear that?"

"If Madame prefers not, it makes no difference," came the officer's reply.

Mata also refused the cord to bind her hands to the stake. Head held high, she faced her executioners as a man's voice shattered the morning stillness. In the next instant the soldiers raised their rifles, each one gazing down the barrel at the breast of the women a few yards away. Their officer stood to the side, just in their eye-line, his sword hovering in the air.

Forty-one years earlier, Margaretha "Gretha" Geertruida Zelle had been born to a wealthy family in the Netherlands, the only daughter among four children. She grew up resourceful and confident, learning much from observing her brothers and her successful father. But not long into her adolescence Gretha's idyll collapsed when her father's speculation in oil shares left them bankrupt. He walked out on the family, and soon afterwards his wife died and Gretha was sent to live with distant relatives. The decade that followed was dogged by despair. Perhaps in search of a surrogate father, she married a man twice her age, a hard-drinking and abusive officer in the East Indies army, and bore him two children. The family sailed to the Dutch East Indies, where they lived in military garrisons, but it's thought that her husband was so disliked by the locals that a maid poisoned the children. The boy died and the girl was badly harmed.

Gretha divorced her husband in 1902 but he refused to pay his ex-wife any maintenance money. Unable to feed her young daughter, she had no choice but to send the child to live with her father in the Netherlands. Not willing to give up hope, Gretha moved to Paris to try and earn enough money to take back her daughter, but there were few jobs for young women in the French capital. For a while Gretha scraped a meagre living giving piano lessons and teaching German, but she was soon obliged to accept 'less respectable' work, first as an artist's nude model and then as an exotic dancer. "Don't think that I'm bad at heart," she wrote to an acquaintance. "I have done it only out of poverty." It wasn't long, however, until she realised that she had a talent for dancing. She also had looks, physique and grace, not to mention a gift for invention. Trading on her olive complexion and her years in the Dutch East Indies, she styled herself as an exotic dancer of Indian extraction. To complete the makeover, Gretha took the stage name Mata Hari, an Indonesian expression meaning eye of dawn.

Soon she was dancing in Paris, Berlin and Vienna, her photograph splashed across newspapers around the world. In an interview with the *New York Daily Tribune* in 1905, she spun one lie after another, telling the paper she was born in India to a Javanese mother and had married a Scottish baronet at the age of 15. Mata told the truth in describing the marriage as unhappy, though, but embellished when asked about her art: "I can dance the sacred dances of India," she said, "which were taught me by my mother, who belonged to the dominant caste of the Hindoo [sic] community."

> "SHE MARRIED A MAN TWICE HER AGE, A HARD-DRINKING OFFICER"

Describing Mata as "exceedingly muscular…lithe and agile", the newspaper furnished its readers with an account of her act: "The dance begins in slow rhythms, and gradually becomes highly impassioned. The costume is purely Indian, disclosing the skin, which is profusely ornamented with jewels and slender gold chains. The feet are bare and in her improvisations… she often works herself up into a pitch of excitement and frenzy."

A decade after this breathless description her career was over. The originality of her act had long since faded, its success spawning a series of imitators who, even if they lacked Mata's charisma, could still capture the allure of the dance. Nonetheless, she had enjoyed a good run, performing for private audiences in European cities and crossing the paths of rich and influential men. By the outbreak of war in 1914 and her 38th birthday she had managed to morph from dancer to courtesan.

She was fortunate that, as a Dutch national, she could take advantage of the country's neutrality to travel freely across Europe, reputedly taking the opportunity to visit her many lovers. Such a position made her an attractive proposition for both German and French intelligence services. The first approach was made in the summer of 1916 by Captain Georges Ladoux of France's Deuxième Bureau, who Mata described as "tall and fat". He offered her 1 million francs in return for information on Crown Prince Wilhelm, the son of the German Kaiser and a man for whom she had danced before the war.

Money wasn't the only incentive for Mata to accept the offer; her favourite lover, a Russian fighter pilot called Vadim Maslov, had recently been shot down and

ABOVE Mata Hari's risqué act disgusted and delighted polite European society in equal measure

ABOVE Margaretha, 21, (front row, far left) on board the ship bound for the Dutch East Indies in 1897, with her new husband behind her

LEFT Gretha's invention of Mata Hari enticed some of the wealthiest and most powerful people in Europe

MATA HARI: SPY OR SCAPEGOAT?

The birth of MI5

BRITAIN'S SECURITY SERVICE SEALED THE FATE OF MATA HARI

Britain's first Secret Service Bureau was established in 1909, but following the outbreak of World War I it split into the Directorate of Military Intelligence, Section 5 (MI5) and Military Intelligence, Section 6 (MI6). The head of MI5 was Captain Vernon Kell, and he and his team of agents pursued the many German spies who were operating in Britain. In total they captured 65 of the 120 agents sent to Britain by Germany and little important intelligence was sent back to Berlin. Such was the extent of MI5's counter-espionage work during WWI that their staff increased to over 800 agents, several of whom were women. MI5's suspicions about Mata Hari led to her subsequent arrest in France, and few in Britain had much sympathy for her. Germany had shot a British nurse in 1915, Edith Cavell, for treason, so the death of Mata Hari evened the score in British eyes.

ABOVE British nurse Edith Cavell was executed for treason by the Germans in October 1915 to worldwide outrage

Spying through the ages

RIGHT John Thurloe, known as Oliver Cromwell's spymaster, established a nationwide network of spies in the 1650s

Espionage has been a military weapon for at least 1,000 years. It was said that King Harold employed spies during his short-lived reign as king of England, but it wasn't for another 600 years that intelligence became an organised branch of a monarch's army. The man responsible was John Thurloe, the spymaster for Oliver Cromwell in the years after King Charles I and his forces had been defeated in the English Civil War. Thurloe planted spies in the most unlikely of places, including the mathematical genius John Wallis, who became arguably the world's first code-breaker, deciphering messages sent between Royalist dissidents.

If some spies relied on brains, others deployed bravado or beauty. In the American Civil War, Rose O'Neal Greenhow spied for the rebel Confederates, using her charm and good looks to extract information from Union officers. Working for the other side was a Welshman called Pryce Lewis, who dressed as an English nobleman and toured the rebel states in a luxurious carriage, fooling Confederate officers over a glass of port into divulging information to the sympathetic Briton. One of Lewis' fellow Union spies was an Englishman called Daniel Webster; he was caught by the rebels in 1862 and hanged. Execution has been the fate of many spies caught behind enemy lines, although the Hague Regulations of 1907 state that "a spy taken in the act shall not be punished without previous trial."

Of the 31 German agents brought to trial in Britain in World War I, 12 were executed, with all but one of the unfortunate spies shot at the Tower of London. With the technological advances of the 20th century, spying grew ever more sophisticated, but the punishments remained the same – when Soviet general Dmitri Polyakov was caught spying for the United States in 1988 he was subsequently executed.

"THE BRITISH COMMUNICATED THEIR SUSPICIONS THAT PERHAPS THE DANCER WAS NOT ALL SHE SEEMED"

was recovering in a French military hospital. Spy for us, posited Captain Ladoux, and access to Maslov will be arranged. Within a few weeks Mata was in Madrid, in the company of the German military attaché, Major Arnold Kalle, requesting a private audience with the Crown Prince. It was during this time that suspicions began to surface about exactly where her loyalties lay.

She had first come to the attention of Britain's intelligence services, the recently formed MI5, in November 1915 when her ship from the Netherlands docked at Tilbury in Essex. She was searched and questioned, and although nothing incriminating was found by the authorities, a letter was sent to MI5 declaring: "She is regarded by police and military to be not above suspicion and her subsequent movements should be watched." When Mata returned to England the following year, she was interrogated for three days by MI5, and although she said she was in the pay of the French secret service, her "contradictory statements" led the British to put her on a boat to Spain with a message circulated that "should she again return to the United Kingdom she was to be detained."

While the British communicated their suspicions to their French counterparts that perhaps the dancer was not all she seemed, she arrived in Madrid and went straight to the German embassy. By now the Germans were also harbouring doubts and a trap was set for her. It sprang shut when she passed some false information about submarines that had been fed to her by Major Kalle on to Captain Ladoux. When Kalle learned of Mata's deceit, he radioed Berlin that their spy, code-named H-21, was a double agent. The coded message was intercepted by a French listening station in the Eiffel Tower and subsequently decoded by British cryptographers in Room 40 of Admiralty Arch. A further message revealed the name and address of H-21's maid – who also happened to be Mata's maid.

She was arrested in her hotel on the Champs Elysées in Paris on 13 February 1917, and after five months stewing in the grim Saint-Lazare Prison, she stood trial on charges of spying for Germany. The evidence against her was weak. She admitted taking money from the Germans but denied that she had divulged classified information, ridiculing suggestions she was indirectly responsible for the deaths of 50,000 French soldiers. As for the phial of invisible ink that Captain Ladoux claimed had been discovered in her hotel room, Mata said it was nothing of the sort and was actually part of her make-up.

The British and American press joined in the farrago, claiming the woman on trial was indeed one of the war's most dangerous spies. According to the New York World, she "spent some time in an English town where the first

ABOVE Saint-Lazare prison in Paris, where Mata Hari was imprisoned between her arrest and trial

ABOVE The Nivelle Offensive in April 1917 to break through the German defences on the Western Front ended in French failure

'tanks' were being made," and subsequently had passed on crucial information to the Germans about their design, "resulting in the enemy rushing work on a special gas to combat their operations". It was nonsense.

In truth, Mata might have passed on inconsequential gossip about life in France to the Germans, but she was guilty of nothing more than that. MI5 described her in its report as a "demi-mondaine", a harlot, and in a telegram to Major Anson of MI5, a member of the British Mission in Paris wrote: "Captain Ladoux, who had the case in hand, tells me that they found nothing incriminating among her effects and nothing to show that she had been in any way connected with espionage in England. During her interrogation she divulged nothing." Yet after a trial that lasted just two days, the dancer was found guilty and sentenced to death. "C'est impossible!" she reportedly cried when informed of the verdict.

What Mata didn't know was that France needed a victim. The war was going badly, and a major offensive on the Aisne in April had failed, prompting widespread mutinies among soldiers. It would strike a further blow to the nation's morale if the notorious spy Mata Hari was found 'not guilty'. She had to die, if only for the sake of French propaganda and pride.

British reporter Henry Wales was one of the few journalists present at the execution of Mata Hari on

BELOW An inaccurate depiction of Mata Hari's execution from a 1920 film

MATA HARI: SPY OR SCAPEGOAT?

15 October 1917. He couldn't help but marvel at her composure as she stood at the stake waiting for death.

"She did not die as actors and moving picture stars would have us believe that people die when they are shot," he wrote. "She did not throw up her hands nor did she plunge straight forward or straight back. Instead she seemed to collapse. Slowly, inertly, she settled to her knees, her head up always, and without the slightest change of expression on her face."

Margaretha Geertruida Zelle's life was over. Abandoned by her father, abused by her husband and exploited by three intelligence agencies, she went to her death with dignity and courage. The woman who had played so many parts over the years saved her greatest performance till last.

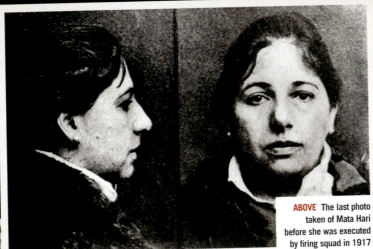

ABOVE The last photo taken of Mata Hari before she was executed by firing squad in 1917

Tricks of the trade

WWI WAS ONE OF THE FIRST CONFLICTS IN WHICH TECHNOLOGY WAS USED TO SPY ON THE ENEMY, AND BOTH SIDES CAME UP WITH SOME INGENIOUS RUSES TO OUTSMART THEIR ADVERSARY

Bird's eye view
A German doctor invented 'pigeon cam' in 1908, creating a harness and breastplate to secure the camera to the pigeon. During WWI pigeons flew over British lines and the camera would take photographs using a pneumatic system time delay.

Tree trickery
Observation post trees were used by Germany and Britain on the Western Front to spy on each other. Built using iron and canvas, the hollow tree stumps could accommodate a man, whose job it was to observe enemy activity during the day and report back at night.

Room 40
Room 40 was the name given to the team of British code-breakers based in the Admiralty Old Building, who, using a captured German code book, successfully decoded some 15,000 of the enemy's secret communications during WWI.

Telephone taps
Germany had a unit of 'telephone troops' on the Western Front in WWI who eavesdropped on British phone conversations by detecting the electrical signals as they went through the ground and amplifying them on high-powered listening sets.

Vanishing act
Secret agents of both sides used invisible ink in WWI to pass messages. German spies made their ink using powdered aspirin mixed with pure water, while another reliable recipe was lemon juice and potassium, which would reveal the message when heated.

PUPPET OF THE RISING SUN

From nationalist hero to servant of the occupying Japanese, Wang Jingwei's efforts to play both sides incurred the wrath of his fellow Chinese

WORDS | EDOARDO ALBERT

On 7 July 1937, Japan invaded China. The Second Sino-Japanese War was the longest phase of World War II, lasting until the surrender of Japan on 2 September 1945, and it was an extraordinarily brutal conflict even by the bloody standards of the wider conflict. Somewhere between 15 and 22 million people died during the bloodshed. But even amid all this brutality, one incident stood out: the Rape of Nanjing. Following the Imperial Japanese Army's capture of the city, Japanese soldiers conducted a campaign of murder and rape that left hundreds of thousands of women dead and tens of thousands of women brutally assaulted.

So it came as the most dreadful shock to the Chinese – who were continuing to fight against the Japanese invasion – when three years later one of the great heroes of China – a leader of the Nationalist movement that had overthrown the old Qing Dynasty – announced that he was to be the head of a new government overseeing the Japanese-controlled parts of China, including Nanjing.

This hero was Wang Jingwei (4 May 1883 – 10 November 1944). He had been a close comrade of the Nationalist hero, Sun Yat-sen, who led the revolution that overthrew the Qing Dynasty in 1911, putting an end to 3,000 years of Imperial Chinese history and pushing China into the modern world. Following Sun Yat-sen's death, Wang Jingwei became one of the two main leaders of the Kuomintang, the nationalist party that Sun Yat-sen had founded along with his great rival, Chiang Kai-shek. Their rivalry ostensibly ended in 1932 when Wang became president of the Kuomintang while Chiang retained control of its army.

Wang was committed to an ideal of Pan-Asianism, the belief that Asian countries had to band together to withstand Western imperialism. However, this belief was sorely tested as, during the 1930s, he began to see that the greatest immediate threat to China was posed by Japan. While Chiang was committed to resisting the Japanese, Wang came to believe that the better course was to come to an agreement with the Japanese since he did not believe the Chinese had the military strength to withstand Japanese aggression. However, Chang was determined to resist.

Despite the losses the Chinese suffered during the Japanese invasion, Chiang retreated with his army, resolved to continue the struggle. Wang was not prepared to support his Kuomintang colleague in this strategy, and on 18 December 1938, Wang and his closest colleagues left what remained of China, flying to Hanoi in Vietnam with the aim of finding some other avenue to peace. It turned out the road to peace went by way of betraying his people.

From Hanoi, Wang made a call for a negotiated peace with Japan, and in May 1939 he flew secretly to Japan to start talks with the Imperial Government. From Japan he went to Shanghai, which was occupied by the Japanese, and signed a secret pact with the occupying power.

On 30 March 1940, Wang became head of the Reorganized National Government of China. This 'national' government happened to control those parts of China that were under Japanese occupation – so it's not hard to see why Wang's regime was quickly labelled collaborationist, rather like the one headed by Marshal Pétain in Vichy, France. Indeed, the only governments that recognised his regime were those that had signed the Anti-Comintern Pact: Germany, Japan, Italy, Hungary, Manchukuo and Spain.

To support his government, Wang also founded a new iteration of the Kuomintang, but his plans were weakened when one of his key Kuomintang supporters defected to Chiang's version of the Kuomintang, taking with him the text of the treaty Wang had signed with the Japanese.

The Kuomintang press immediately branded Wang a traitor and proceeded to excoriate him. For his part, Wang attempted to gain greater autonomy from the Japanese, although he only succeeded when the war in the Pacific turned against them in 1943 and the Imperial Government

BELOW Wang Jingwei was a noted orator and an accomplished poet; implicated in a plot to assassinate the heir to the Qing throne, his courage at trial led to his sentence of execution being commuted to life imprisonment

ABOVE Wang Jingwei raises a toast with Heinrich Stahmer, Nazi Germany's ambassador to China, 1942

needed to free up men to stem the American advance. However, this increased latitude came too late for Wang's government to be able to do much to establish itself as the Japanese grip on China weakened.

Throughout his four years in charge of part of China, Wang remained committed to three principles: Pan-Asianism (his government portrayed the war as China and Japan against Anglo-American imperialism), anti-communism and virulent hostility to Chiang Kai-shek's regime. But the Japanese had little use for his Pan-Asian views, the Chinese communists were biding their time, and Chiang Kai-shek could see the tides of war turning against the Japanese. All he had to do was wait.

He did not have to wait too long. In 1939, while in Hanoi, Kuomintang assassins had attempted to kill Wang. Although he had survived the attack, complications from it meant that he fell ill early in 1944. He flew to Japan in March for treatment, lingering on until 10 November 1944. His body was taken back to China and buried close to the mausoleum holding Sun Yat-sen. However he was not destined to rest in peace. Following Japan's defeat in the war, Chiang Kai-shek's forces took control of Shanghai again. They removed Wang's body from its tomb and burned it before destroying the tomb itself. A pavilion was later erected on the site on which Wang is noted as a traitor.

To this day, most Chinese remember Wang Jingwei as a traitor, although some who endured the horrors of Japanese occupation did assert that his regime reduced their sufferings. But such small revisions have done little to change his reputation.

LEFT In a war remarkable for its brutality, the actions of the Imperial Japanese Army following their capture of Nanjing stand out as especially depraved

The 'What If' Newspaper

Cambridge   Interview by Callum McKelvie   1950

CAMBRIDGE SPY RING APPREHENDED

A Soviet spy ring recruited at Cambridge University has been discovered after one of its members dropped secret documents while leaving a pub

EXCLUSIVE Interview With

ANDREW LOWNIE

A graduate of Cambridge himself, Lownie founded his own literary agency in 1988 and is the author of a number of titles including *Stalin's Englishman: The Lives of Guy Burgess*, *The Mountbattens: Their Lives and Loves*, and *The Traitor King*, a biography of Edward VIII.

Who were the Cambridge Five?
The Cambridge Five were five undergraduates recruited in Cambridge during the 1930s. They're normally regarded as Kim Philby, Donald Maclean, Guy Burgess, Anthony Blunt and John Cairncross, but this is a slight misnomer as there were many other students recruited by the Russians at Cambridge and other universities during the 1930s. The Russians called the group the Magnificent Five because they all knew each other and were very closely connected. Guy Burgess, for example, had affairs with both Donald Maclean and Anthony Blunt at Cambridge, a bit like the Bloomsbury set, which I think is why everyone is so interested in them. There was a sort of romantic or sexual connection as well as a more public one.

What information did they pass on?
They all passed on enormous amounts of information because they all had

John Cairncross, pictured in 1990

OUTRAGE AS BLUNT SIGNS SOVIET FILM DEAL

Soviet film producers have signed a 25-film contract with art historian/spy Anthony Blunt. The series will follow Anthony's adventures as he faces off against a slew of super-villains bent on world domination. The series will also feature high-octane chase sequences in reasonably priced government-sponsored cars, the glamour of a lack of consumer goods and the thrill of Anthony rambling about antiquarian art.

THE CAMBRIDGE SPY RING

Anthony Blunt

Donald Maclean

Guy Burgess

Kim Philby

The 'What If' Newspaper

extremely important roles. Burgess worked for the BBC and put forward speakers who were sympathetic to the Soviet Union, like Anthony Blunt. Later, in the Far East Department, he helped shape British policy to recognise Red China. He then worked as a private secretary to the deputy foreign minister, where he basically saw everything, not least sensitive intelligence documents. He took stuff to the Russians, who photocopied them, then Burgess returned them the next morning. We know that from 1941 to 1945, Burgess passed 4,604 documents to the Russians. The result was during the Four Power Conferences and post-war reconstruction of Europe, the Russians knew the British position often before the British negotiators knew themselves. This was crucial for things like the Berlin airlift.

It's not just documents, either. Burgess would lend his flat for assignations, particularly to colleagues who were ostensibly married with children but who were homosexual. He gave this information to the Russians, who might then use it to blackmail them.

Then there was Maclean, who was involved in atomic energy planning. A damage assessment for the U.S. Joint Chiefs of Staff in October 1955 said that planning on atomic energy and U.S./UK post-war policy in Europe was all totally compromised. The view was taken that everything that crossed the spies' desks from the time they became active in 1935 to the time they were caught in 1951 was compromised.

This material was so important that people like Stalin, particularly during the war, thought the Cambridge Five were triple agents. Cairncross was at Bletchley, so he knew all about Enigma and he was able to tell the Russians. Blunt was a very high official in MI5 and Philby was a career MI6 officer. The irony is that when the Americans discovered Maclean, the first person they spoke to about it was Philby, so he was able to tip off Maclean.

Why did it take so long for the fourth and fifth members to be exposed?
Well, they were in fact all suspected in 1951. If you look at the investigations (and the papers are now in the National Archive) Philby, Blunt and Cairncross were all questioned. MI6 were prepared to give Philby the benefit of the doubt, and he was allowed to work as a sort of freelancer until he fled in 1963, so he probably had access to secret information until then. Blunt was also suspected, but there was not enough evidence until another spy came forward in 1964. He was given immunity until 1979, when Mrs Thatcher was forced to name him publicly. With Cairncross, again pretty much all the evidence was found in 1951 but he was allowed to pursue an academic career, first in America and then in Italy, and it was only espionage writers in the 1980s who revealed his treachery.

As Macmillan said, "When my gamekeeper shoots a fox I don't bring it into the drawing room, I bury it in the garden." And that was what they did.

How much evidence is there that there were other members?
We have various bits of evidence. We know that after Philby was recruited in Vienna he went back to Cambridge with a list of seven people he was targeted to recruit. Number one on the list was Donald Maclean and number seven was Guy Burgess. What we don't know are the numbers two to six, whether they were approached and turned him down or whether they were recruited. We also know that when the Russians recruited spies they numbered them, and we know from the files that there's a big gap in the numbering between Maclean and Burgess, even though they were recruited only a few weeks apart.

Another bit of evidence is the broken Venona codes, which revealed spies called Professor, Poet and Chauffeur – we just don't know who they are. Finally, there were many people who were investigated who either partially confessed or there was no evidence and who were allowed to basically retire.

Trinity College, where four of the five were recruited

Anthony Blunt confessing during a television broadcast

Kim Philby during a press conference where he admitted he was guilty

THE CAMBRIDGE SPY RING

How close did each member come to being captured? Were there specific instances?

Yes, there were. Burgess liked to meet his Russian controller in the pub, and there was one instance when his suitcase filled with secret documents fell open. A kindly policeman, not realising how sensitive they were, helped put them back. Another time, Burgess and Blunt had documents in a suitcase and were stopped by the police. The police thought they were burglars, but when they didn't discover any tools for breaking into houses they were let off.

How could the group have been prosecuted?

The interesting thing is that George Blake was prosecuted just a few years later and sent to prison, so there seemed to be two rules: one for people who went to public school and another for people who didn't. The ostensible reason was that they didn't have the evidence to bring a case under the Official Secrets Act and to do so they would reveal they'd broken Soviet codes. But I think there wasn't the will there. There was a discussion at one point that Burgess could be prosecuted if he came back to Britain, but that was just a bluff as they wouldn't have been able to do it. It suited the government's purposes to have Burgess, Maclean and Philby in Moscow and for Blunt and Cairncross to have their immunity and keep quiet.

What was the effect of the Cambridge Five on British intelligence?

It was pretty devastating. They didn't know what was compromised, whether agents they had recruited had been betrayed and whether information was true. It subsequently led to witch hunts against intelligence officers. Indeed, a man called Guy Liddell probably would have been head of MI5 but because of his friendship with Burgess he was sacked. Public respect for institutions of government was affected too. The phrase 'The Establishment' was coined in a *Spectator* editorial in which they describe the white paper on Burgess and Maclean defection as the 'Whitewash Paper'. We feel we're distrustful of the government now, but one of the earliest things that shook faith in government institutions was this scandal.

> "We know that from 1941 to 1945, Burgess passed 4,604 secret documents to the Russians"

What would have changed had they been caught earlier?

If they'd have been caught earlier lots of things that were betrayed wouldn't have been betrayed, including agents and operations. There wouldn't have been the extent of demoralisation, there wouldn't have been the lack of cooperation, and intelligence would have operated far more effectively in terms of safeguarding British interests. It's impossible to say how things would have been different. The USSR had an advantage not only in diplomatic negotiations but also in an assessment of our intelligence and military capabilities.

How would Anglo-American intelligence relations have changed?

There would have been greater cooperation, especially on nuclear intelligence matters. That relationship was restored, and I think it did continue in a modest way because we were joined to the Americans and their need, for example, for our bases abroad. But there was a lot of suspicion, particularly from the FBI, and there were a lot of turf wars between various government agencies in America, as well as between America and Britain. It was embarrassing and damaging, but because a lot of the stuff remains secret we don't know what was and wasn't shared, and it's difficult to do an audit as there are so many variables we just don't know about.

Would their capture have had any wider implications for the Cold War?

Yes, it would've stopped them giving away secrets, not least Burgess in the Far East Department and who was heavily involved in the Korean War. American lives might have been saved and there might have been a different outcome. If they hadn't been caught when they were Philby and Maclean might've gone to the top and done a lot more damage. Philby was touted as a future head of MI6 and he would only have retired in 1975 – many years after his treachery was discovered.

THE CAMBRIDGE 50?

There is much to suggest that the Cambridge Five spy ring was just the tip of the iceberg and the Soviet penetration of British intelligence was far deeper. More contemporary research suggests there was another ring at Oxford University as well as attempts to recruit people at LSE, Imperial and Birmingham University. This was part of a Soviet plot to develop moles within a range of government institutions, which could then be activated later on and used for long-term information gathering. There were also a number of individuals who were investigated and either partially confessed or there was not enough evidence. These included Michael Straight (part of the American ring), Alister Watson (an individual who worked within the Admiralty) and a senior civil servant called Dennis Proctor. "Just because we know about the ones that have been discovered doesn't mean that there were not lots of others," says Lownie.

The Soviets recruited spies at the heart of government

WANTED: PATRIOTIC HELP FOR GARDENING SURVEY

Do you work in an important government institution? Do you like the planting of flowers? At Hammer & Sickle Gardening Tools we look to expand our patriotic brand of Excellent Capitalist Equipment by asking you a few questions. Our survey asks simple questions like: Where do you work? Who's your boss? What are the cipher codes? What's your favourite rose? (Red is best). If interested, meet in the alley off Fleet Street and when asked for a match reply, "No, but I have a lighter."

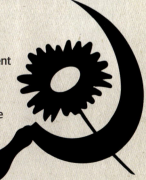

EPHIALTES OF TRACHIS

The betrayal behind the legend of the 300 Spartans

WORDS | CHRISTOPHER EVANS

Ephialtes of Trachis is widely regarded to be the most infamous traitor in Greek history. His name even translates into 'nightmare' in English today. But it would be difficult to understand the magnitude of Ephialtes' betrayal and his role in the Battle of Thermopylae without being aware of the events and the years that led up to it.

During the Greco-Persian Wars between 492 BCE and 449 BCE, the Persian Empire was the most powerful in the world, as well as one of the largest in history, reaching all the way from Egypt to India.

At this time Greece was made up of various city-states, some situated in Asia Minor, a peninsula of land connecting Europe with Asia. These city-states included Athens, Corinth, and Sparta.

The Ionian Greeks, who were under Persian control, rose up in revolt in 499 BCE over dissatisfaction with taxes and the meddling of various tyrants who feared repercussions from the Persian Empire. Although the uprising was quickly quashed, King Darius, leader of the Persians, was furious with the other Greek city-states who had lent their support to the Ionians' cause. Determined to punish them, Darius set into motion the first Persian invasion of Greece.

What should have been an easy win for the Persians, who outnumbered the Athenian army greatly, became a humiliating defeat that took place at Marathon Bay. The Persians lost over 6,000 soldiers compared to the Greeks' 192. They retreated quickly and headed to Athens, hoping the element of surprise would help them gain ground in their campaign. Legend has it a lone messenger was sent to Athens to warn them of the oncoming danger. The messenger ran the entire way, inspiring the name of the marathon races held today.

King Darius was dead, but his heir, Xerxes, took up his mantle and continued his father's campaign against the Greeks. Thirsty for revenge, Xerxes amassed an enormous army and fleet and began what would be the second invasion of Greece. It was a slow process; the Persians lost many warships during a storm and spring turned to late summer before any real progress had been made.

Although normally rivals, Athens and Sparta, the most powerful city-states in Greece, once again put their differences aside in the face of the incoming Persian invasion. Led by King Leonidas of Sparta, the Greek army, estimated to have been made up of 7,000 men, decided to meet the enemy at Thermopylae. This was a narrow pass in the mountains that could barely fit a wheeled cart, so Xerxes' men would be forced into a bottleneck that would give the Greeks the upper hand. For two days this worked, and the Greek force managed to defend their position, pushing back against the Persian army despite being outnumbered by 100 to one (or, according to some accounts, 300 to one). Unfortunately for the Greeks, one of their own would make a decision that would result in their undoing.

Although much of Ephialtes' life is lost to history (his origins trace back to Trachis, a town in which the Greek tribe the Malians resided), the story of his betrayal is recounted by Greek historian Herodotus in his work *The Histories*, which details the Greco-Persian wars.

According to these accounts, Ephialtes saw the chance for a reward from the Persians, and with the promise of great riches, he told Xerxes about a little-known pathway that cut through the mountains. This information allowed the Persian army, with Ephialtes leading the way, to bypass the Greeks at Thermopylae and ambush them from the other side.

Outflanked and outnumbered, Leonidas ordered the majority of the Greek army to retreat, keeping behind only 300 Spartans with him to face the Persians who, according to all accounts, slaughtered them quickly. Leonidas' head was cut from his dead body as a final insult.

After his betrayal, fearful of the Spartans' repercussions, Ephialtes fled to Thessaly with a price on his head and no reward from the Persians. Ten years later he was murdered in an unrelated incident, though the Spartans still paid their bounty to his killer in recognition of his deed.

While his true motive remains unknown, in the 2006 film *300*, Ephialtes is shown as a disfigured man who was raised in exile by his parents in order to spare him from being murdered for his deformities. He appeals to Leonidas to allow him to join the Greek phalanx, but the king has no choice but to refuse him because Ephialtes is physically unable to hold his shield high enough, which would be fatal to the strength of the formation. Aggrieved at being denied the chance to help, Ephialtes betrays his countrymen.

RIGHT The Persian force was vast, yet the Greeks had been holding it off

EPHIALTES OF TRACHIS

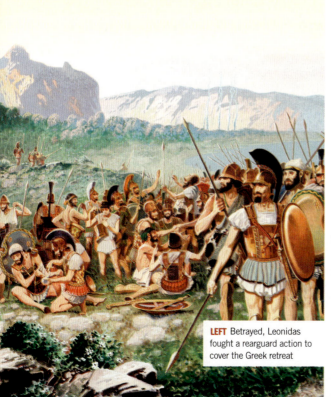

LEFT Betrayed, Leonidas fought a rearguard action to cover the Greek retreat

RIGHT A view of the ancient battlefield of Thermopylae as it looks today

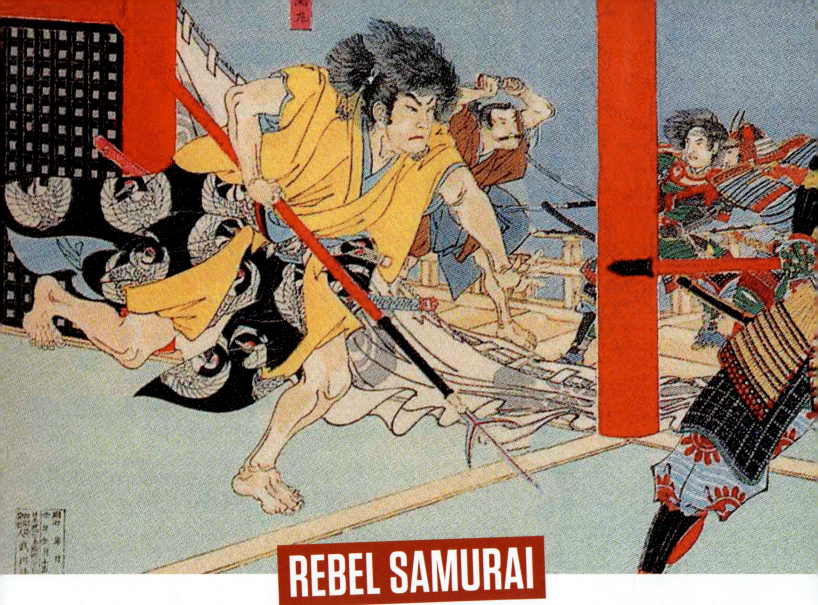

REBEL SAMURAI

AKECHI MITSUHIDE

In 16th-century Japan, one famed samurai shocked the imperial court with his unexpected revolt

WORDS | GREG KING

Akechi Mitsuhide was born in 1528 and is said to have been a member of the powerful and influential Toki clan. Japan was then in the Sengoku period, a time of warring factions and fierce samurai who constantly fought for influence and power. From childhood he was trained in warfare by Saito Dosan, known as the "Viper of Mino". Mitsuhide nearly lost his life in 1556 when Dosan's son overthrew his father and tried to eliminate his allies. His men destroyed Akechi Castle, Mitsuhide's ancestral home, forcing Mitsuhide to flee for his life. After a period in exile he entered the service of Oda Nobunaga in Kyoto. Nobunaga was the most powerful and ruthless warlord, or daimyo, in Japan and was attempting to wage a war of political unification in Japan. At the time Japan was mired in a series of seemingly endless clan wars. Nobunaga had destroyed the powerful Takeda clan, and he now began a sustained assault on the two remaining rival clans, the Mori and the Uesugi. After proving himself in a number of important victories, Nobunaga trusted Mitsuhide implicitly. Beginning in 1570, Mitsuhide launched the Omi campaign east of Kyoto. Following his victory there he was rewarded with lands in Sakamoto, where he later built a castle.

In June 1582, Nobunaga ordered Mitsuhide to take his army and join Toyotomi Hideyoshi in a siege against the Mori clan in Chugoku region. Mitsuhide had an army of some 13,000 soldiers. Nobunaga planned to join Mitsuhide, but before doing so he stopped at Honno-ji Temple in Kyoto. Having already sent most of his soldiers on to join

AKECHI MITSUHIDE

LEFT The Siege of Honno-ji Temple in Kyoto

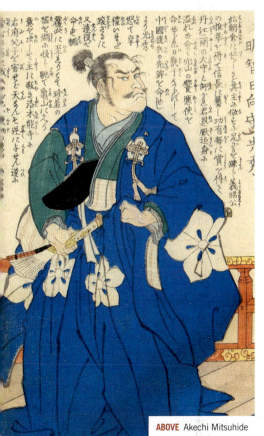

ABOVE Akechi Mitsuhide

the battle, Nobunaga was left with just 150 guards, along with courtiers and servants. Even so, Kyoto was under his control, and he had no reason to fear for his life. Honno-ji boasted fortified walls and was surrounded by a moat, which gave the erroneous impression that it was safe from a siege.

But Mitsuhide, aware that Nobunaga was largely unprotected, decided that this was the moment to stage a coup d'etat against his master. His reasons for doing so remain lost to history. It was a dramatic turn against the samurai honour code. There has been speculation that Mitsuhide had grown tired of his subordinate position under Nobunaga, who consistently treated him poorly and humiliated him in front of others. Perhaps he simply wanted power. But it is also likely that revenge played a part. In 1579, Mitsuhide laid siege to Yamaki Castle and promised its lord, Hatano Hideharu, that he would be safe if he surrendered; as a guarantee, Mitsuhide even handed Hideharu his own mother as a temporary captive. But Nobunaga ignored this agreement. When Hideharu surrendered, Nobunaga had him killed. In revenge for this betrayal, Hideharu's supporters executed Mitsuhide's mother.

Mitsuhide's soldiers were loyal to Nobunaga, and so he did not reveal his plans to anyone except his most trusted officers. When the men arrived in Kyoto it was a rainy morning. On the orders of their superiors, they laid siege to Honno-ji temple, unaware that Nobunaga was holed up inside. A surprised Nobunaga at first thought that the noise came from a street fight, but on learning that Mitsuhide was attacking, he seemed resigned to his grim fate.

Grabbing a bow and quiver of arrows, he rushed to the walls of the temple and began firing at the attackers. When he ran out of arrows he snatched up his spear. Wounded in the arm, he fled to an inner room as flames began engulfing the building. Precisely how Nobunaga died is not known, but it is thought that he committed seppuku (ritual disembowelment) to evade capture.

Mitsuhide bragged that he was responsible for Nobunaga's death. He urged the Oda clan vassals to recognise him as shogun. The imperial court, shocked by Mitsuhide's rebellion, refused to support him, and he was forced to flee Kyoto. One of Nobunaga's loyal generals, Toyotomi Hideyoshi, gathered some 20,000 troops and set off in pursuit of Mitsuhide, who had fled to the nearby mountains at Settsu. His own men began to desert him, and by the time Hideyoshi caught up with him south of Shoryuji Castle only a fraction of his men remained.

Mitsuhide and his troops faced Hideyoshi at the Battle of Yamazaki but were quickly overwhelmed. Mitsuhide fled, hoping to reach the protection of Sakamoto Castle, but he was killed by a farmer who was hunting for fallen samurai.

LOVE THY BROTHER

Was George Plantagenet a drunken, grasping schemer, or did he fall victim to a case of sibling rivalry gone too far?

WORDS | BEE GINGER

When it comes to historical biographies, that of George Plantagenet could easily be likened to a plot from *Game of Thrones*. His story is filled with betrayal, treachery and feuding families that left a bloody mark on British history.

George Plantagenet came into the world on 21 October 1449 in Dublin, Ireland. His father, Richard of York, 3rd Duke of York, and mother, Cecily Neville, were delighted to welcome another boy into their expanding family. George was their ninth child born in ten years, and it was quickly apparent to those that encountered him that he had his father's hunger for power coursing through his veins.

At the time of George's birth his father was lord lieutenant of Ireland for King Henry VI. However, this lofty position was not enough to sate his desire for greater status, and it would be Richard's attempts to acquire the throne that aided in bringing about the Wars of the Roses, a brutal struggle between the houses of York and Lancaster that spanned over 30 years and left thousands dead.

Since his first breakdown in 1453, Henry VI had lapsed into bouts of serious mental illness, rendering him unfit to rule. In his stead a group of powerful barons governed England, chief among them Richard of York, who possessed a strong claim to the throne given that he was a descendant of King Edward III. However, Henry's wife, Margaret of Anjou, was no wallflower and deftly exploited rivalries among the barons in an effort to maintain control. Eventually these tensions boiled over when Richard was excluded from the royal court. Determined to avenge this grave insult, Richard took up arms on 22 May 1455 at the Battle of St Albans, sparking the Wars of the Roses.

The whole Plantagenet family became embroiled in the conflict, which took a turn against Richard and the rebels in 1459 after the Battle of Ludford Bridge. This defeat forced Richard to flee to Ireland and his son Edward to run for Calais in France. Meanwhile, Richard's wife, Cecily, was captured at Ludlow Castle along with their sons George and Richard. They were later released, and after initially being relocated to Fotheringhay Castle with his mother and siblings, George was placed in the custody of his aunt, Anne, Duchess of Buckingham.

As the war raged on, Richard used his connections to the king to gain Henry's trust. Handily for Richard, the king's health was rapidly declining and he was often in a confused or catatonic state, making him all the easier to 'advise'. While Richard's attempt to seize the throne by force failed, in October 1460 a compromise was reached in the form of the Act of Accord. This made Richard the heir to the throne, and shortly afterwards he was granted further status and influence by being named as lord protector. However, his jubilation was short-lived.

Refusing to back down, the Lancastrians marched on Sandal Castle, Richard's stronghold, in December of the same year. For reasons that still remain a mystery, Richard and his men sortied out from their safe haven and were annihilated at the Battle of Wakefield on 30 December 1460. Richard and his son Edmund both perished in the fighting, and their heads were later displayed for all to see on the top of the Micklegate Bar in York, a paper crown placed upon Richard's in mockery of his ambitions.

LOVE THY BROTHER

Following his father's death, George was taken into exile in Burgundy with his younger brother, Richard. Here they resided with the Duke of Burgundy, who kept the boys at arm's length. At the age of only 11 George had seen first hand how unpredictable life could be. Thankfully for George, his luck was set to take a turn for the better when his older brother, Edward, crushed the Lancastrians at the Battle of Mortimer's Cross on 2 February 1461, before repeating the feat at the Battle of Towton on 26 March, to this the day the bloodiest waged on English soil. The throne was back in Yorkist hands.

The pendulum continued to swing in George's favour, as, once back in England, he was awarded the title of Duke of Clarence and was chosen to be lord lieutenant of Ireland following his brother's coronation in June 1461. He also became the heir presumptive to the throne, a position he would hold for nine years. Yet despite Edward's generosity,

BELOW Richard Neville, Earl of Warwick, was known as the Kingmaker

BOTTOM The Duke of Clarence languishes in the Tower of London awaiting his fate

George grew into a resentful, petulant young man obsessed with retaining his right to power. It was this sense of entitlement that led him to betray his brother.

In 1464, Edward was married to Elizabeth Woodville, a union that displeased George immensely as it put at risk his place in the line of succession. It was at this point that he joined forces with his first cousin on his mother's side, Richard Neville, Earl of Warwick, son of the late Earl of Salisbury, who had died alongside Richard of York at the Battle of Wakefield. Warwick, who had helped Edward to take the crown, was equally appalled by the union given Elizabeth was both a Lancastrian and held no royal rank, and the marriage drove a wedge between him and the king.

Relations soured further in 1497 when Edward removed Warwick's brother, George, from his position as chancellor, and the situation worsened again in 1469 when Edward refused to allow Warwick's daughter Isabel to marry George, thereby preventing George from acquiring any independent wealth through marriage, meaning he would have to remain beholden to Edward. This simultaneously dashed Warwick's dreams of Isabel one day birthing a child that would sit on the throne. This was the second time Edward had forbidden a union for George; he had previously wanted to tie the knot with Mary of Burgundy, another affluent suitress. It would seem George had a type.

George was apoplectic with rage, but with the help of Richard, who secretly arranged a papal dispensation on the grounds that the pair were first cousins, the two were married in Calais in July 1469 without Edward's knowledge. Coincidently, embarrassing rumours began to circulate about the king that suggested his marriage was invalid and his children were illegitimate.

Warwick and George were now in open rebellion, and after an army loyal to Warwick defeated a royal host at Edgecote, the pair arrested Edward. However, they were soon forced to liberate the king when it became clear that sympathy for their cause had faded. Remarkably, this wasn't the end of their treachery.

Unable to recover his former influence over the king, Warwick decided to install George as king and stirred up another rebellion in 1470, this time in Lincolnshire. A rebel army of some 30,000 men led by Sir Robert Welles met King Edward and his troops in Rutland in the East Midlands on 12 March. The royal army carried the day, cutting down the rebels, who threw off their coats as they fled in an effort to rid themselves of the colours of Warwick and Clarence. The site of the battle therefore came to be known as Losecoat Field.

Among the debris littering the battlefield, some papers were discovered that revealed Warwick and Clarence's involvement in the uprising. Left with no other choice, the pair fled to France, aligning themselves with Margaret of Anjou and putting their weight behind yet another bid to restore Henry VI to the throne. In this they were successful, forcing Edward into exile in Flanders and reinstating Henry in October. But George's allegiance with the Lancastrians and Warwick was not to last.

In return for his new pledge of allegiance, Henry VI made George next in line to the throne behind Henry and Margaret's son, Edward. However, Warwick then arranged for his daughter Anne to marry Edward, a move that, assuming the union produced children, nullified the reward Henry had given to George. Realising his cousin no longer planned to help him take the crown, George reached out to his brother. Staggeringly, Edward agreed to a reconciliation with the caveat that George was to have no more to do with Warwick or the House of Lancaster.

Back in the fold, George strove to have his brother reinstated, and on Easter Sunday 1471 he took to the field alongside his brothers at the Battle of Barnet. Warwick met them at the head of a force of 15,000, approximately 3,000 more soldiers than Edward commanded. He had the numbers, but Mother Nature had other ideas. Confused by a thick layer of fog, Warwick's army attacked itself, allowing Edward's men to surround and destroy it. Warwick was slain in the fighting.

Before Edward's return to England, Warwick had attempted to engineer his daughter Anne's (George's sister-in-law and a widow since the death of Prince Edward at the Battle of Tewkesbury in 1471) marriage to Richard of Gloucester, George's younger brother. Unsurprisingly, George, who wished to claim the Neville estates by treating Anne as his ward, tried to meddle in the planned union, even sending Anne into hiding disguised as a maid. But the marriage went ahead with the blessing of Edward, enabling Richard to claim half of Anne's inherited estates.

Further woe befell George in December 1476 when Isabel died a few months after childbirth. Despite the precise cause of death being unknown, George, in a state of abject paranoia, accused his wife's lady-in-waiting, Ankarette Twynyho, of poisoning her. Despite the absence of any proof, she was tried by a jury that had been coerced by George into handing out a guilty verdict and hanged. This was aristocratic corruption at its finest, as George had no authority to mete out such a punishment.

When Edward found out too late what had happened he began to worry greatly about his brother's state of mind. Either as a warning or in retaliation for Twynyho, Edward had John Stacey, a member of George's household, executed for the crime of imagining the king's death using sorcery. Outraged, George made the grave error of asking a Lancastrian friend to march into Parliament and declare Stacey's innocence of the crime. Such rank insolence, coupled with his earlier crimes, left the king with no other choice than to have George arrested on a charge of high treason and incarcerated in the Tower of London.

George's trial took place in January 1478 and was overseen by Edward. The jury learned how George had plotted against his brother and even accused him of using witchcraft to poison some of his subjects. Condemning George's "unnatural, loathly treasons", Edward ordered Parliament to pass an act of attainder against George.

On 18 February 1478, at the age of 28, George was privately executed in the Bowyer Tower. It remains uncertain whether or not he was beheaded, a traditional form of execution for nobility. Rumours have circulated ever since his death that he was drowned in a vat of sweet malmsey wine, possibly at the duke's request – a final dig at his brother's alcoholic tendencies. Buried at Tewkesbury Abbey, his remains were later exhumed and showed no signs of a beheading, which begs the question, did he in fact endure a more unique ending?

LOVE THY BROTHER

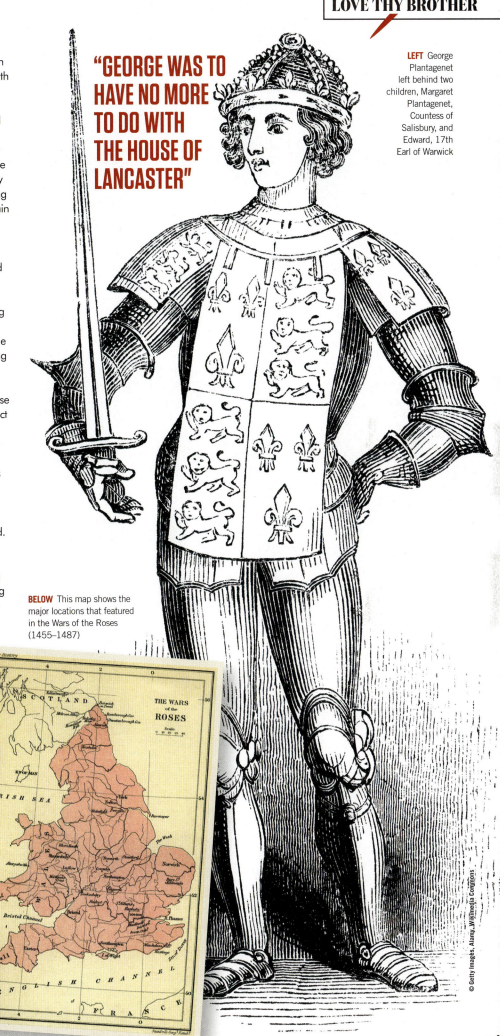

"GEORGE WAS TO HAVE NO MORE TO DO WITH THE HOUSE OF LANCASTER"

LEFT George Plantagenet left behind two children, Margaret Plantagenet, Countess of Salisbury, and Edward, 17th Earl of Warwick

BELOW This map shows the major locations that featured in the Wars of the Roses (1455–1487)

TALLEYRAND

His name became a byword for treachery, but was Charles-Maurice de Talleyrand-Périgord the great betrayer, or was he himself betrayed?

WORDS | APRIL MADDEN

The elderly gentleman had a gift for uniting even the worst of enemies. Not through reason, or diplomacy, or appealing to their higher selves – though he had been a master at all of those in his day. Not through silver-tongued persuasion, even though this remained his greatest gift. No, as the old lush went hobbling through the pretty winding streets of Saint-Florentin, on his way – so the gossips said – to an assignation, a brothel or the bed of another man's wife, he united those he passed in hatred. The Catholic with the Protestant, the republican with the monarchist, the Bonapartiste with the Bourbon restorationist, even the English with the American; they drew themselves into little knots of hatred and spite as he stumbled by, they spat in his wake and whispered, "Le diable boiteux!" ('The lame devil') behind his back. Worse things had been said to his face – Napoleon had called him "shit in a silk stocking". He had been many things in his colourful life, walked many paths and worn many faces. To one faction or another, each of those faces was that of a traitor. But was this true of the man behind the masks?

Charles-Maurice de Talleyrand-Périgord was born on 2 February 1754 into an aristocratic family. It was not, however, a wealthy one. His parents, Charles-Daniel, comte de Talleyrand-Périgord, and Alexandrine de Damas d'Antigny, were both from noble houses, but as the youngest child of their respective families they had little more than their names to show for their illustrious heritage. Alexandrine was a courtier, and Charles-Daniel a lieutenant-general in the French Royal Army, so the young Talleyrand was sent off to be looked after by a nursemaid. It was she that he blamed for what he claimed was an injury that left him lame for the rest of his life – he claimed the nursemaid ignored him falling off a chest of drawers and breaking his ankle – although later historians think it much more likely Talleyrand had a congenital disability instead. Whatever the case, the childhood nurse paid no attention to the young Talleyrand's worsening limp, and it was only after his great-grandmother, Princess de Chalais, sent for the boy that his condition was discovered. Talleyrand later wrote that Madame de Chalais was "the first member of my family who displayed any affection for me, and also the first who taught me the sweetness of filial love". If he thought there would be an outpouring of parental affection due to his lame leg, he was mistaken – what rights and expectations he had as his father's eldest living son and heir-presumptive were promptly transferred to his younger brother when Talleyrand's disability was discovered. He was just four years old.

His great-grandmother, however, loved the boy and worked to instil in him the aristocratic French idea of noblesse oblige – that with nobility and wealth comes the responsibility to look after others. She was famous for how she treated the peasant folk on her estate: every Sunday after mass, the princess invited her people into what she called her "dispensary" in the chateau, where she would examine and treat illnesses and injuries using medicines made to her own recipes. Throughout his long life, Talleyrand would return in memory to the time he spent at Chalais, contrasting his great-grandmother's treatment of him with that of his parents. He would brood constantly, too, on what he believed, or certainly claimed, was the accident that had caused his disability and how it had affected his life. In later years, he would realise that it had actually saved him from a violent death during the French Revolution: he had not been seen to be a member of the notoriously indolent, dissipated royal court at Versailles. His father had, in fact, withdrawn the boy's rights as his eldest surviving son because he was horrified by the idea that a teenage Talleyrand, presented to the king to ask the royal favour of a position in the army that was his right as a noble, would be seen to limp through the august corridors of the royal palace. Instead, Talleyrand was destined for the only career his father believed was open to him: the church. At the age of just eight, the golden idyll of his Chalais childhood was over. Another betrayal was added to the tally.

His father did not bother to escort the young Talleyrand to the Collège d'Harcourt that was now to be his home; that duty was left to an ageing retainer. Even here, Talleyrand was rejected as an outcast; his disability meant that he couldn't join in the sports and roughhousing of his fellow boys, leaving him forever aloof. Here, he tried to convince himself that his mother and father had little time for him – he was escorted to a desultory and largely silent Sunday dinner with them once a week – to spare them the heartbreak of losing a beloved child to Holy Orders. In fact, what his parents hoped was that he would succeed his prestigious uncle Alexandre Angélique to the throne of the Archbishopric of Reims, adding more wealth to the family coffers and prestige to the family name.

Talleyrand was ordained in 1779, and fewer than ten years after that, consecrated Bishop of Autun. But Talleyrand had a secret: since his time in the seminary, he had been reading texts that criticised both church and state, texts that would be key in fomenting the revolution that was about to shake France. Just three years after attaining his bishopric he would resign it, abandoning Catholicism to the extent that Pope Pius VII would eventually strip him of Holy Orders.

It's here that Talleyrand's reputation for treachery began, with his casting-off of religion. In pre-revolutionary Catholic France, this was heresy of the

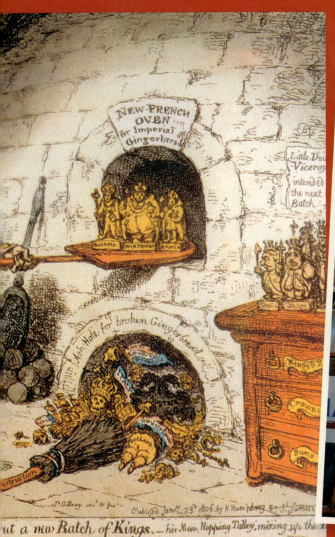

highest order. But Talleyrand went further than that: he joined the voices agitating for the wealth of the French church to be redistributed to the nation and its people, even proposing a bill that would seize its goods and lands, as well as the personal possessions of wealthy clergymen, like his uncle, using the proceeds to provide poor relief – an early welfare benefit paid in food, clothing or money – to ordinary French folk that needed it. Other legislation he was involved in caused the French church to schism entirely, with one underground faction loyal to the pope in Rome while the mainstream church was under the control of the state. Monastic vows, orders and monasteries were banned. Talleyrand didn't just reject Catholicism on his own behalf, he attempted to completely dismantle it.

Talleyrand was now highly placed in revolutionary politics, so much so that he was tasked with a vital, though unofficial, diplomatic mission. Visiting London in 1792, his objective was to persuade the increasingly alarmed British not to declare war on France. Initially, he succeeded, winning a declaration of neutrality from British Prime Minister William Pitt the Younger. Talleyrand was a talker, not a fighter, but despite his service to the cause, this didn't stand him in good stead with the increasingly desperate revolutionary leadership. In September 1792, with a force of royalist French expats and their Prussian allies bearing down on Paris in the wake of the fall of the French monarchy the month before, the newly republican French state took the momentous decision to execute anyone who refused to fight for the First French Republic. Talleyrand sweet-talked a passport out of the minister of justice, Georges Danton, and fled to Britain. By December of that year, the revolutionary government he had once served issued a warrant for Talleyrand's arrest.

For a couple of years, Talleyrand was safe in Britain, but tensions with its increasingly volatile neighbour across the English Channel were rising. Britain's monarchy feared that the French revolutionary fever would spread to their own subjects, and with war between the two inevitable, Talleyrand was expelled from Britain. He set off for the United States. While initially he worked as a bank agent, Talleyrand's innate ability to gravitate towards movers and shakers soon saw him meet and befriend the likes of Benedict Arnold, Aaron Burr and Alexander Hamilton. He swore his oath of allegiance to the U.S. before the mayor of Philadelphia in May 1794, but two years later, he was back in France, taking advantage of the more moderate attitudes that followed in the wake of the arrest and execution of the notorious Maximilien Robespierre.

Talleyrand was now foreign minister, and he busied himself with international trade. The war between Britain and France was having a chilling effect on American trade, and the U.S. Government, conscious that

OPPOSITE An 1815 caricature of Talleyrand as 'the man with six heads'

ABOVE, LEFT A caricature by the famous British cartoonist James Gillray depicts Talleyrand and Napoleon as gingerbread makers baking up a fresh batch of French kings

ABOVE A blue plaque in Mayfair, London, showing where Talleyrand lived when on the run from his former allies

Talleyrand was a former ally and an American citizen, thought that he would perhaps be a better negotiation partner than the Britain they had seceded from. They were wrong. Talleyrand demanded a hefty bribe from his former friends before he would even consider opening negotiations. His stance would result in an unofficial maritime conflict called the Quasi-War in which French naval and American trade ships attacked each other on the sea routes between Europe and the New World.

But Talleyrand had bigger fish to fry than the U.S. merchant fleet. A coalition alliance of Russia, Austria and a host of smaller Italian states was on the attack, provoked by the revolution and France's annexation of Savoy and Nice, which had originally been part of Piedmont-Sardinia. Talleyrand began correspondence with a brilliant young Corsican commander and came to believe he would be a better hand on the reins of power than the current government. By 1799, Talleyrand was one of Napoleon Bonaparte's most influential advocates and supported the coup that brought him to power as first consul in 1799.

In 1804, Napoleon crowned himself emperor, but by then Talleyrand was tiring of his protégé. He had disagreed with the decision to sell what is now the state of Louisiana to the fledgeling United States and, on a more personal level, had been offended by Napoleon's autocratic insistence that he marry his long-term mistress, Catherine Grand. By 1807, he was tendering his sympathy to European rulers whose nations Napoleon had attacked, and it didn't take long before he was betraying Napoleon's secrets wholesale to them. By 1815, Napoleon had been removed from his throne by yet another coalition of European nations and the Bourbon monarchy restored to power, Talleyrand having convinced his new allies that France would return to its pre-Napoleonic borders in exchange for their promise not to annex new territories from it. In recognition of this, the new king, Louis XVIII, appointed Talleyrand to a ceremonial role, one which paid well but left him unfulfilled. Napoleon made a brief return to power that year before his final defeat, and after that, France enjoyed a modicum of peace until the death of Louis XVIII and the accession of his younger brother, Charles X.

TALEYRAND PERIGORL PRINCE of BENEVUNTUM

Charles was an ultra-royalist. He wanted to return France to the god-fearing, feudal, punitive state it had been before the revolution and set about dismantling the civil liberties of the First French Republic. As far as Talleyrand was concerned, he had to go, and he was a driving force in the July revolution that toppled Charles X's rule, using as his mouthpiece a newspaper – Le National – that he had been instrumental in setting up. Charles X abdicated in favour of his nine-year-old grandson, but the crown ultimately ended up on the head of Charles X's cousin, Louis Philippe, the so-called Citizen King. He would be the last master Talleyrand would serve, and he served him well: in 1834, now ambassador to Britain, Talleyrand brokered an alliance between France, Britain, Spain and Portugal. He resigned and retired the same year, splitting his time between the Chateau de Valençay and the little town of Saint-Florentin.

He wrote his memoir, recounting his feelings of betrayal at the hands of his parents and the French aristocratic system that had rejected him, the church that had confined him, the revolutionaries who had turned on him, the emperor he had raised up who had spurned his knowledge and experience, the resurgent Bourbon monarchy who had disappointed him. He fretted over his legacy in the wake of the cult of Napoleon and the wars that beset Europe. Most of all, he fretted over the country he said he had only ever sought to guide, prop up and protect. Talleyrand was famous for cannily and selfishly switching his allegiance between many masters, but according to him, he had only ever served one mistress – France herself.

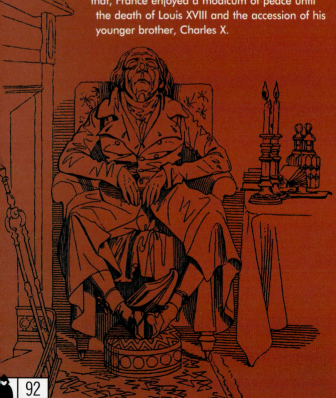

ABOVE Talleyrand is depicted as wise (the owl) but treacherous (the snake)

LEFT A 19th-century drawing of the elderly Talleyrand. In his last years he lost the ability to walk

"TALLEYRAND FRETTED OVER HIS LEGACY IN THE WAKE OF THE CULT OF NAPOLEON"

TALLEYRAND

Talleyrand in his bishop's mitre (on the right) in the early days of the French Revolution

THE INFAMOUS LORD HAW-HAW

How did an American-born Anglo-Irish fascist become the English voice of Nazi propaganda in World War II?

| WORDS | GREG KING |

Wars always bring out traitors, and World War II was certainly no exception to this rule. Some of the worst offenders were propagandists hired by the Third Reich and their allies to espouse the depraved views of fascism, Tokyo Rose and Axis Sally just two of the most well-known. But few were as notorious as William Joyce, the most famous of the Nazi sympathizers who broadcast from Germany in World War II using the name Lord Haw-Haw.

Joyce was born in Brooklyn, New York, to Irish émigré parents in 1906. When he was three his parents returned to Ireland. During the Irish uprisings and battle for independence, Joyce supposedly acted as a British Army informer. In 1922, following Irish independence, the family moved to England, where Joyce studied History and English Literature at Birkbeck College.

The same man who spent his teenaged years as a British Army informer underwent a remarkable political metamorphosis in his late twenties. Increasingly he came to believe that Britain was under the rule of an international Jewish cabal that was intent on destroying the country. He absorbed right-wing views and joined Sir Oswald Mosley's British Union of Fascists. The two men repeatedly clashed, and in 1937 Mosley expelled Joyce from the Union. On 24 August 1939, when war seemed inevitable, Joyce fled Britain, taking up residence with his wife, Margaret, in Berlin.

RIGHT A crowd gathers outside Wandsworth Prison to see a notice pinned up announcing Joyce's execution, 3 January 1946

THE INFAMOUS LORD HAW-HAW

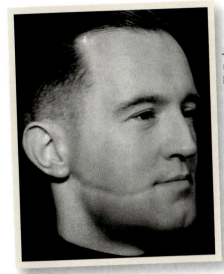

ABOVE Joyce was scarred for life when a communist slashed him with a razor during a Conservative Party meeting

RIGHT Joyce became a German citizen in 1940 and was later awarded the War Merit Cross by Hitler – who he never actually met

Nazi Minister of Propaganda Joseph Goebbels had established a radio programme, *Germany Calling*, broadcast principally to Britain and meant to undermine Allied morale during the war. After brief stints by several men at the microphone, Joyce took over in the continuing role of Lord Haw-Haw. The name had come from a *Daily Express* journalist, who wrote in September 1939 that the broadcaster "speaks English of the haw-haw, dammit-get-out-of-my-way variety… I imagine him having a receding chin, a questing nose, thin yellow hair brushed back, a monocle, a vacant eye, a gardenia in his buttonhole. Rather like PG Wodehouse's Bertie Wooster."

The broadcasts immediately attracted a large audience. Haw-Haw was sardonic, sly and mocking, and his programme regularly offered reports on the fate of Allied soldiers, making the broadcasts potentially a source of primary information. But the underlying messages were twofold: Jews were responsible for the war and Britain should surrender and make peace with Germany. Allied ships that were sunk, Allied planes that were shot down, Allied losses on the battlefield – all were diligently reported in an effort to discourage the war against Germany. The aim was to make Britons feel that the war was a losing battle.

Joyce made his last broadcast on 30 April 1945 – the same day on which Hitler later committed suicide along with his wife, Eva Braun, as the Red Army encircled Berlin. "And now I ask you earnestly," he said, "Can Britain survive? I am profoundly convinced that without German help she cannot." Unaware of the drama that was taking place inside the bunker in the heart of the Third Reich as he continued to exhort his listeners on Germany's behalf, Joyce ended his broadcast with, "Heil Hitler!"

At end of the war in Europe, Joyce and his wife fled to a small village near the Danish border. On 28 May, two British officers spotted Joyce; one was Horst Pinschewer, a German-Jewish refugee who went by the name Geoffrey Perry who, suspecting that Joyce might be armed when he reached into his pocket, shot him in the leg. Joyce was arrested and turned over to British military police.

Joyce was charged with three counts of high treason. His defence argued that, because he was an American citizen, Joyce couldn't be convicted of any offense against the Crown. But Joyce had lied about his nationality to obtain a British passport, and the court decided that the charges against him were valid. At trial he was acquitted of two charges but convicted on one count: "Being a person owing allegiance to our Lord the King and while in a war being carried out by the German Realm against our King, [Joyce] did traitorously adhere to the King's enemies in Germany, by broadcasting propaganda."

"In death as in life," Joyce said after his conviction (which he appealed), "I defy the Jews who caused this last war, and I defy the power of darkness which they represent. I warn the British people against the crushing imperialism of the Soviet Union. May Britain be great once again… I am proud to die for my ideals and I am sorry for the sons of Britain who have died without knowing why."

On 3 January 1946, Joyce was hanged at Wandsworth Prison, and his body was buried in an unmarked grave. In 1976, his surviving daughter gained permission to have him exhumed and his remains were buried in County Galway, Ireland.

STRONGMAN OF BURKINA FASO

Implicated in politically motivated murder, Blaise Compaoré participated in a coup d'etat that led to the downfall of a lifelong friend

| WORDS | MICHAEL E. HASKEW |

Thomas Sankara, the first president of Burkina Faso, was an avowed Marxist and revolutionary known to the Burkinabé people as their own personification of legendary Argentinian freedom fighter Che Guevara. He had come to power in the impoverished West African nation – formerly known as Upper Volta – in an August 1983 coup d'etat and immediately set about transforming his country.

That regime overthrow had been supported by the governments of neighbouring Ghana and Libya and accomplished with the help of a few close associates. Among those political activists and government officials who boosted Sankara to power were army officers Major Jean-Baptiste Lingani and Captain Henri Zongo, but most prominent was the president's long-time comrade Blaise Compaoré.

Compaoré was born in Ziniaré in central Upper Volta on 3 February 1951. As a child he attended a Catholic school before spending some time in a *lycée* (college) in Ouagadougou (today the capital of Burkina Faso). Tragically, his mother died when he was just 15 (his father would pass away a few years later), and he was later expelled from college. His attention turned towards a military career, and in time he became close with Sankara, whose father, Joseph, embraced him like one of his own.

As his military career progressed, Compaoré led troops in parachute and commando training and commanded an army regiment. When Sankara resigned a government post in opposition to prevailing policies and was thrown in jail, it was Compaoré who ignited a revolt, secured the revolutionary leader's freedom and ensured the success of the coup. Thereafter, Compaoré held the posts of minister

STRONGMAN OF BURKINA FASO

ABOVE Thomas Sankara was just 37 when he was murdered. He was warned about a potential plot against him but refused to believe Compaoré would betray him

OPPOSITE Granted citizenship in Ivory Coast in 2016, Compaoré, now 73, continues to live in exile

BELOW Kosyam Palace, the official home of Burkina Faso's president, is located in Ouagadougou. Currently, the country is ruled by Ibrahim Traoré, who took power in a coup in 2022

of state at the presidency and minister of state for justice, effectively serving as the second most powerful man in Burkina Faso.

But all was not well in the halls of power. By 1987, Compaoré, Lingani and Zongo had become disenchanted with Sankara's leadership. Despite the president's popularity with the masses, the treacherous triumvirate launched a coup of their own on 15 October. On that dark day, Sankara was attending a meeting with fellow West African government officials in Ouagadougou when a team of assassins attacked, spraying Sankara and 12 others with bullets. The leader's corpse was quickly buried in an unmarked grave while his wife and children were forced to flee the country.

Compaoré was quick to deny any involvement in the horrendous attack, claiming that he was grieving his close friend, with whom he had attended a party just five days prior to the shooting. But his supposed grief didn't prevent him from snatching power and publicly stating that Sankara's policies had jeopardized relations with neighbouring countries and with France, the region's former colonial ruler and its most influential European ally. Further, he claimed that Sankara had been scheming to assassinate political opponents.

In 1989, Compaoré was himself the target of a coup spearheaded by none other than Lingani and Zongo. His former collaborators had bided their time until the president was out of the country and then hatched their plan to topple him. However, their scheme was uncovered and the pair, along with two other conspirators, were promptly arrested and executed. Compaoré capitalised on the plot to restructure the government.

Compaoré would rule for 27 years, and during his tenure he implemented a number of left-wing programmes, befriended Libyan strongman Muammar Gaddafi, supplied arms to guerrilla movements in West Africa and sought to further the economic development of Burkina Faso through warmer relations with countries around the globe.

Willing to alter his perspective on the world and his policies to curry favour, Compaoré was also seen at times by the United States Government as a friend in the restive region. He pursued an agenda of economic liberalisation and limited democratic reforms, and Burkina Faso adopted a new constitution in 1991. All the while, however, he remained intent on holding power.

In the same year as the new constitution was adopted Compaoré was elected to a seven-year term as president. Re-election followed again in 1998, 2005 and 2010, in part because opposition was so fractious and political parties so numerous that a cohesive coalition could not be formed against him. Of course, there was some conjecture as to the validity of the election results.

In time, the disenchantment of the Burkinabé people with his rule became readily apparent, and many bristled at the 1998 death of journalist Norbert Zongo – a prominent anti-Compaoré voice – under suspicious circumstances.

Economic hardships and mounting mistrust of the Compaoré regime sparked protests on numerous occasions, and political opponents questioned the legality of another term as president in 2005, claiming term limits forbade it. Successfully bypassing this and other attempts to curb his personal power, Compaoré announced in 2014 that he planned to abolish term limits through a constitutional amendment. This was the last straw.

Violence and demonstrations broke out across Burkina Faso in October as an estimated 1 million disaffected protesters took to the streets and government buildings were set ablaze. The unrest forced the president to resign from office on the 31st. He fled the country and found sanctuary in Ivory Coast, and a transitional government was installed.

The ouster, however, was not the last that the world would hear regarding the exiled former president. In April 2021, a full 34 years after the assassination of Thomas Sankara, a Burkinabé military tribunal charged Compaoré and 14 others with complicity in the murder. He was tried in absentia and found guilty not only of complicity in Sankara's death but also with endangering state security and the concealment of Sankara's corpse. In April 2022, he was sentenced to life in prison. Compaoré is believed to still reside in Ivory Coast, out of reach of justice – but not the ire of his people.

SIR ROGER CASEMENT: BRITISH TRAITOR, IRISH HERO

What led an Anglo-Irish diplomat knighted by King George V to betray Britain?

WORDS | GREG KING

On 6 July 1911, Anglo-Irish diplomat Roger Casement was knighted by King George V. Five years later, he was hanged as a traitor. It was a spectacular fall, one fueled by his anti-imperialism, attempts to secure Imperial Germany's support for Irish independence, and by his homosexuality.

The irony is that, for most of his life, Casement had been very much a member of the British diplomatic establishment, working for the Foreign Office. Born outside Dublin in 1864 to a Protestant regimental captain and a Catholic mother, he had been appointed as a consular representative in French Congo. He began resenting colonialism, although he continued diplomatic service in Portugal and Brazil until he retired in 1913, returning to his native Ireland.

By this time Casement had identified himself with the cause of Irish independence, having previously joined the Gaelic League, which promoted the Irish language. In 1913, he joined in the formation of the Irish National Volunteers. "It is a mistake for an Irishman to mix himself up with the English," Casement wrote. "He is bound to do one of two things – either to go to the wall [be shot] if he remains Irish or to become an Englishman himself."

In August 1914, as WWI began, Casement went to New York to meet Count Bernstorff, the German ambassador to America. Casement suggested that if Germany sold Irish separatists guns the men would then rebel against British rule, thus diverting troops from the war against Germany. Casement followed this with a trip to Germany, where he obtained a promise that the Kaiser's government would not invade Ireland and would, in the event of a German victory, let the country decide its own destiny.

Although Germany had agreed to arm the Irish nationals, their shipments were intercepted by the British, who were warned that there might be a rising in Ireland at Easter, 1916. A German U-boat brought Casement back to Ireland on 21 April. Knowing that the rebels would lack sufficient arms, he tried to stop the Easter Rising, but he was suffering from a recurrence of malaria and was unable to do so. He was arrested by the Royal Irish Constabulary three days after his arrival and sent to London for trial on charges of high treason and espionage. The Crown faced one difficulty: the Treason Act of 1351 covered only activities on British soil, while Casement had undertaken his efforts overseas. The court eventually amended its interpretation of the act to allow for Casement's prosecution.

The trial at London's Old Bailey in the summer of 1916 lasted just four days. It took the jury only an hour to find Casement guilty. On hearing the sentence, Casement addressed the court, arguing that he could not be guilty of treason against England because he was Irish. He decried colonialism, "Where men must beg with bated breath for leave to subsist in their own land, to think their own thoughts, to sing their own songs. Surely it is a braver, a saner, and a truer thing to be a rebel… I went down a road that I knew must lead to the dock." His actions, he concluded, were "based on ruthless sincerity".

His conviction garnered much attention, and notable luminaries George Bernard Shaw, W. B. Yeats and Sir Arthur Conan Doyle asked that the verdict be overturned or that his life be spared. To combat this, British intelligence showed Casement's diaries to King George V, newspaper editors and influential officials. As these chronicled Casement's homosexuality, he was depicted as an amoral deviant unworthy of reprieve.

Casement was hanged at Pentonville Prison on 3 August 1916. "He appeared to me the bravest man it fell to my unhappy lot to execute," the hangman later said. Casement's body was stripped and he was tossed naked into a prison grave next to the infamous Dr. Crippen.

Although the Irish Government spent decades asking its British counterpart to return Casement's remains to their country for proper burial, this was refused until 1965. When the coffin arrived in Dublin, it lay in state for five days in the Garrison Church at Arbour Hill. A funeral with full military honours was then held before Casement was laid to rest in Glasnevin Cemetery. Irish President Éamon de Valera was among the 30,000 mourners. In a driving sleet, he eulogised Casement: "It required courage to do what Casement did, and his name would be honoured, not merely here, but by oppressed peoples everywhere, even if he had done nothing for the freedom of our own country."

OPPOSITE To this day, some researchers are adamant that the diaries used to convict Casement were forgeries

ALCIBIADES
THERE AND BACK AGAIN

The life of Alcibiades is a fascinating story of deceit, cunning, power, and greed

WORDS | MARK DOLAN

There are perhaps more well-known names among the ancient Greeks than from almost any other ancient culture: Socrates, Plato, Aristotle, Pericles, Aspasia, Pythagoras, Hippocrates, Alexander, Thucydides, Sappho – the list goes on (though with notably few women appearing, it must be said). One whose name is perhaps not immediately provocative but who certainly sparked some strong opinions among his contemporaries is the politician and military leader Alcibiades.

Born around 450 BCE in Athens but given a Spartan name, Alcibiades might be one of the first people in history to fall prey to a kind of nominative determinism. His father, Cleinias, had fought valiantly in the battles of Salamis (the Greek island, not to be confused with the contemporary Cypriot city-kingdom) and Plataea 30 years earlier, battles that brought to an end the second phase of the Greco-Persian Wars. Unfortunately, Cleinias fared less well in the First Peloponnesian War, being killed in the Battle of Coronea in circa 447 BCE. After his father's death Alcibiades was placed under the care of Pericles, his mother's cousin, but perhaps more importantly also one of the most important politicians in the history of Athens.

It was Pericles who played a central role in bringing Athens to the centre of the Greek world, leading its golden age and helping to develop both Athenian democracy and the Athenian Empire. If that wasn't enough, he also oversaw the construction of the Acropolis, one of the greatest monuments of the ancient world. Pericles evidently had his hands full, and unfortunately for young Alcibiades, parenting didn't rank as highly on his list as making Athens the premier power of the Mediterranean. Pericles' partner at this time was Aspasia, an Ionian courtesan who was also renowned as a great wit and thinker. Plato records that Aspasia even had a huge influence on Socrates' thinking and rhetoric, and it is likely that she met the young Socrates when she first came to Athens in around 450 BCE.

ALCIBIADES: THERE AND BACK AGAIN

Clearchus of Soli, a later Cypriot philosopher, wrote that Aspasia had consorted with Socrates prior to her relationship with Pericles. Whatever the details of their relationship, Socrates certainly knew and respected Aspasia.

It was likely this relationship that led to Socrates becoming acquainted with Alcibiades, who had grown into a strikingly handsome young man. Socrates was drawn to the young man's mind and body alike (Alcibiades' beauty was legendary; he had many lovers of both genders and is still considered one of the most beautiful men of the time), but it was not until Socrates saved Alcibiades' life in the Battle of Potidaea in 432 BCE that their relationship blossomed.

Socrates' heroics in this battle would have lasting effects. After the battle was over the Athenian generals were discussing to whom they should award the aristeia. This was an award taken directly from Homer's works that recognised the greatest warrior, and although Socrates was deserving of the accolade, he refused the honour and it was instead bestowed on Alcibiades.

After this, Socrates became Alcibiades' mentor and the two grew close. The teachings of Socrates certainly had an impact on Alcibiades, but as time went on and his political ambitions grew he eventually moved away from the philosophical virtues that his mentor espoused and engaged instead in the kind of political manoeuvring he derided.

During Alcibiades' formative years Athens had been prospering under the stewardship of his adoptive father, Pericles. In 431 BCE, however, the peaceful years came

RIGHT Alcibiades and Socrates greatly revered Aspasia, the philosopher and wife of Pericles

to an abrupt end with the outbreak of the Second Peloponnesian War. After two years of heightening tensions between Athens and Sparta, Thebes, a Spartan ally, attacked Plataea, an Athenian ally, and fighting broke out. The war brought to Athens not only violence but also a plague that devastated the city and took the life of Pericles. Leadership of the Athenian alliance passed to Cleon, an aggressive and somewhat bloodthirsty leader, at least according to the historian Thucydides. Sparta, suffering from Cleon's aggressive strategy, began to pursue peace, though Cleon was unmoved. The Battle of Amphipolis in 422 BCE changed the picture entirely, as both Cleon and Brasidas, the equally pro-war Spartan general, were killed. Nicias, now in charge of the Athenian alliance, negotiated a peace, to the relief of both sides and their depleted resources.

Alcibiades, though, took umbrage with the treaty. He thought that the Spartans should, given his family's historical role in Athenian-Spartan diplomacy, have come to him rather than Nicias to discuss the peace treaty. Taking advantage of his renown as an orator, his relationship to the late Pericles and the tension surrounding the fragile peace, Alcibiades seized the moment.

OPPOSITE Socrates saved the life of the young politician Alcibiades in the Battle of Potidaea

RIGHT Socrates became Alcibiades' close friend, mentor and probable lover

BELOW A map of the Athenian and Spartan alliances at the beginning of the Second Peloponnesian War

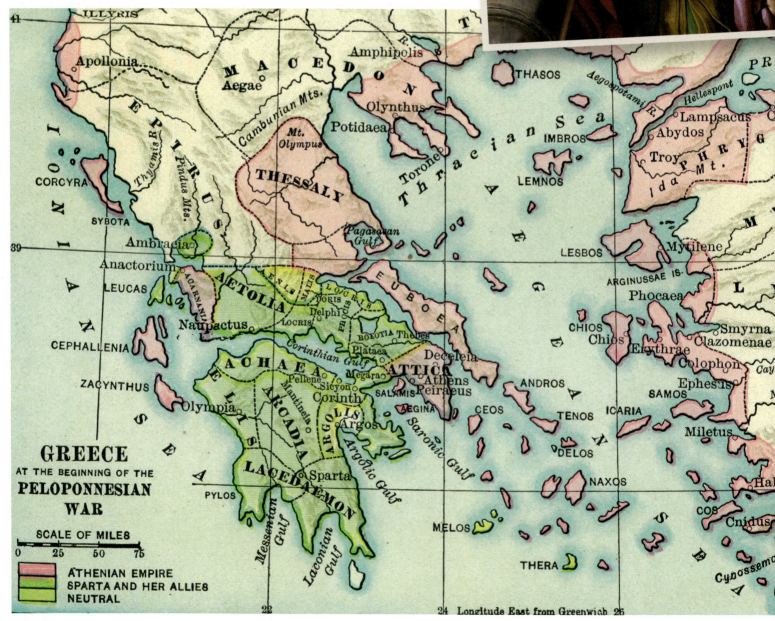

ALCIBIADES: THERE AND BACK AGAIN

By 420 BCE, Alcibiades had risen to the rank of general and was directly opposing Nicias. Unsatisfied with the result of the first part of the Second Peloponnesian War (the Ten Years' War), partially because of personal reasons, he led Athens into an alliance with Argos, Elis and Mantinea in 419 BCE. These Peloponnesian states were dissatisfied with what they saw as Sparta's capitulation to the Athenian alliance. Sparta was left with no choice but to fight Athens, and this new mini alliance, needing to prove to the rest of the Peloponnese their continued military strength. Sparta emerged victorious, saving its reputation but damaging that of Alcibiades.

This loss put him in danger of ostracism (the word ostracism derives from *ostraka*, the shards of pottery used as voting token) – exile via public vote. The vote was orchestrated by another of his political rivals, Hyperbolus, who also put forward Nicias as a candidate for ostracism. His scheme backfired; Nicias and Alcibiades decided to temporarily put aside their differences and got Hyperbolus successfully ostracised instead.

Alcibiades' next move was perhaps his most consequential. Displeased with the position Athens and its allies found themselves in, and eyeing his perceived destiny as an Achilles-esque Homeric hero, he convinced Athens' leaders to pursue expansion into Sicily. The Athenians had been asked in 416–15 BCE to come to the aid of the Sicilian city of Segesta, which was facing aggression from another Sicilian city, Selinus, itself supported by Sicily's largest city, Syracuse. It was argued that, through a network of allies, if Syracuse were able to take Segesta, it may – as an ally of Sparta – in turn pose a threat to the Athenian Empire. This gave Alcibiades the perfect opportunity to again put into use his oratorical abilities, giving a rousing speech to the Athenian assembly that convinced them that not only would an expedition to Sicily be a chance to prevent Sparta gaining traction, but it would grow the Athenian Empire and win them further wealth and influence.

Nicias was a vocal opponent of the plan, but he was not as convincing as Alcibiades, and so the pair, along with Lamachus, another Athenian general, were appointed to lead the expedition. In fact, Nicias' explanation of what a prohibitively monumental undertaking the expedition would be had the opposite effect from his intention: the Athenians opted to provide the enormous resources Nicias had claimed it would require. It was not only Nicias who was against this move; Socrates wrote to Alcibiades urging him to reconsider, but the young politician's desire for power and glory trumped his loyalty to his former mentor.

Before the expedition could set sail from Pyraeus, Athens' harbour town, an event occurred under cover of night that would change everything. Hermai could be seen throughout Athens, often used as boundary markers. These were stone statues, with the head of the god Hermes and often a phallus at the relevant height, and they were sacred. Just before the Sicilian expedition was due to leave the city's hermai were defaced, a crime ascribed to drunken louts and thought to be a terrible omen for the campaign in Sicily, as Hermes was the god of travellers and would be responsible for ensuring the army's safe passage. Alcibiades' rivals wasted no time implicating him in the heresy, carrying with their accusations the suggestion that he was attempting to overthrow Athenian democracy.

Alcibiades demanded a trial but was refused, with his enemies fearing he would have the support of the army. Instead it was decreed that he would continue to lead the army, and the expedition left Pyraeus. Shortly after leaving, Alcibiades was found guilty of the vandalism, in addition to a second crime of mocking the Eleusian Mysteries, the most sacred and revered cult in Greece. He was ordered to return to Athens and stand trial for his crimes, where, if found guilty, he'd be condemned to death. Alcibiades agreed to return by his own ship but reneged and fled. This was taken as an admission of guilt and he was quickly sentenced to death should he show his face in Athens again.

Instead of returning and facing this fate Alcibiades set course for Athens' great rival, Sparta. On arriving, Alcibiades was able again to exercise influence through his oratorical and rhetorical abilities, claiming that the Athenians were attempting to conquer Sicily before going on to conquer the entirety of Greece and much of the rest of the western Mediterranean. He convinced the Spartans to send support to Syracuse while simultaneously fortifying the city of Decelea a few miles outside Athens. This forced the Athenians to fight on two fronts, with the Sicilian expedition embroiled in a long-term siege of Syracuse and their resources stretched to breaking point. Nicias soon surrendered and was executed.

Alcibiades proved to be a valuable asset to the Spartan alliance as the Peloponnesian War continued. He soon convinced Spartan leaders to allow him to travel to some of Athens' ally states in and around Ionia and foster resentment against Athens by asserting their failures in recent naval excursions and convincing them that the wars in Sicily and Decelea had weakened Athens so much that it was no longer the military force it had once been. In doing so he managed to forge an alliance – albeit not a strong one – between the Spartans and the Persians.

It was not long, though, before Agis, the Spartan king, took against Alcibiades, likely because the latter had seduced – and possibly impregnated – the king's wife. Whatever the reasons, Agis ordered Alcibiades' death. There was, however, a way out for Alcibiades; he fled to join the Persians, befriending the Persian commander Tissaphernes, whom he had previously met. While he was ostensibly working with the Persians, helping them to weaken the Spartans (by letting them and the Athenians wear each other out), he went back to the Athenians with an offer: if they overthrew the democracy and replaced it with an oligarchy, he could get the Persians on their side. This was a deal that appealed to both sides; the Persians found it much simpler to deal with kings or oligarchs than an unwieldy democracy, while Athens gained the support of the Persian army.

Alcibiades' primary aim in this manoeuvre was more personal, however. He believed that by bringing the Persians to Athens' side he could bring about his triumphant return to the Athenian fold. His plan was eventually successful, and the Athenian democracy was overturned and replaced with the short-lived Four Hundred. Before long this small oligarchy was replaced with a more democratic Five Thousand and Alcibiades was recalled by the Athenian navy, who recognised his influence and their need for aid.

On his return, Alcibiades was able to turn around Athens' fortunes and oversee a series of significant victories at the battles of Hellespont, Bosporous and the Sea of Marmara. Such were his achievements that when he arrived back in

"HE BELIEVED THAT BY BRINGING THE PERSIANS TO ATHENS' SIDE HE COULD BRING ABOUT HIS RETURN TO THE ATHENIAN FOLD"

BELOW A herma, one of the sacred statues of Hermes Alcibiades was accused of defacing

ALCIBIADES: THERE AND BACK AGAIN

BELOW A depiction of the Battle of Syracuse, a conflict won by Sparta with Alcibiades' help

ABOVE The death of Alcibiades, Athenian hero and villain

LEFT Alcibiades made a heroic return to Athens years after defecting to its enemies

Athens he was greeted as a hero, all outstanding charges against him were dropped, and he was made *strategos autocrator* (commander-in-chief) and given almost total control of the military.

His luck finally ran out at the Battle of Notium around 408–6 BCE, when the Athenians suffered a comprehensive defeat, leading to his removal from power. Soon after, he saw his successors growing complacent, but his warnings about the dangers of their poor planning were ignored, with devastating consequences. In 405, the Greeks and Spartans clashed at the Battle of Aegospotami, a naval engagement in the Hellespont. Just as Alcibiades had cautioned, a lack of preparation cost Athens dear, its entire fleet wiped out by the Spartan commander Lysander. The war was over.

Alcibiades fled back to Persia hoping to find refuge, but Lysander, having profited from the Athenians' refusal to heed Alcibiades' warning, may have contacted the Persians and arranged to have him murdered. Whether Lysander arranged his fate or not, Alcibiades, a man with many enemies, is said to have died in a shower of arrows.

SELLING OUT THE HANGMAN'S HIT SQUAD

As the Nazis hunted for the assassins who dared to kill Reinhard Heydrich, one Czech resistance fighter decided to rat them out

WORDS | MICHAEL E. HASKEW

Karel Curda had lost his nerve. The Czech radioman who had made a daring parachute drop into his homeland in order to fight against the occupying forces of Nazi Germany was at the end of his emotional rope. Just days earlier, SS Obergruppenführer Reinhard Heydrich, acting reichsprotector of Bohemia and Moravia, had died of wounds received during the execution of Operation Anthropoid, an audacious plot – approved by the Czech government-in-exile – to strike a blow against German high command. Heydrich, the embodiment of Nazi brutality and a man who had earned nicknames including "The Hangman" and the "Butcher of Prague", had been attacked

SELLING OUT THE HANGMAN'S HIT SQUAD

on 27 May 1942 while riding in his Mercedes convertible through the streets of the Czech capital. Gravely wounded in the assassination attempt by an anti-tank grenade hidden inside a briefcase, Heydrich eventually died on 4 June. His assassins, Czech soldiers Josef Gabcik and Jan Kubis, trained in clandestine activities by the British Special Operations Executive (SOE), had been on the run since the attack, and the Nazis were determined to root them out.

Frustrated that their manhunt was proving futile, the Nazis' retribution was horrific. On 10 June, the village of Lidice was wiped off the proverbial map. All men over the age of 15 were summarily shot, while the women and children were sent to a concentration camp. Hundreds more Czech civilians were rounded up, brutalized and executed as part of the drive to find Heydrich's killers. After a few days, Curda, born in October 1911 in the town of Stara Hlina, then a part of the Austro-Hungarian Empire, could take the bloodshed no more. As they searched 36,000 homes in the vicinity of Prague, the Nazis made a public demand for information and offered a reward of 10 million crowns to anyone willing to betray the perpetrators.

In an anonymous letter, Curda wrote to the SS and Gestapo investigators: "Cease searching for the assassins of Heydrich; cease arresting and executing innocent people. I can't stand it any more." He went on to identify the assassins as "…a certain Gabcik from Slovakia and Jan Kubis from Moravia".

Crippled with fear for his own life and probably motivated by the reward, Curda followed the letter with a personal appearance at Gestapo headquarters in Prague's Petschek Palace. So nervous was the turncoat that the Germans could barely understand that he was trying to offer up his former comrades. However, when Curda picked out Gabcik's captured briefcase from a group of several others, he finally got their attention.

Curda told the Nazis that he wanted to stop the killing of innocent people and save his own family – and himself – from retribution. Nevertheless, he was interrogated intensely, beaten and threatened repeatedly with execution. Although he did not know the specific whereabouts of Gabcik and Kubis, he did divulge the locations of several safe houses. One of these belonged to Marie Moravec and her 17-year-old son, Ata. The assassins had sheltered there on more than one occasion in the months leading up to Heydrich's assassination.

Soon enough, the Nazis closed in. Maria committed suicide on the morning of 17 June, and her son was arrested, plied with alcohol and tortured. Finally, the grisly spectacle of his mother's severed head floating in a fish tank broke Ata. He disclosed that Gabcik and Kubis were possibly hiding in the Cathedral of St Cyril and Methodius in central Prague. Indeed, the pair had taken refuge along with other Czech fighters in the church crypt.

After a lengthy gun battle and even an effort to flood the fugitives out of their hiding place, the agents had all either been killed or chosen suicide over capture and excruciating death. When the bodies of Gabcik and radio operator Josef Valcik were dragged onto the sidewalk, Curda positively identified both. As the orgy of Nazi retribution finally subsided, it transpired that 13 members of the church had been executed along with more than 250 friends and relatives of Gabcik and Kubis, while a second village, Lezaky, had been ravaged.

For the rest of the war, Curda collaborated with the Nazis, and he also took a German wife. Some evidence suggests that he had even expressed admiration for Hitler during his special operations training in Britain, but commanding officers in the military gave him good assessments, one even asserting that Curda was "…capable, and understanding, diligent and persistent".

Enigmatic though he was, there is no confusion as to the result of Curda's treachery. Despite his concern over loss of life, hundreds of Czech patriots and innocent people died as a result of his duplicity.

Several top Nazis who perpetrated unspeakable war crimes after the death of Heydrich were brought to justice after the war. Curda, too, could not escape the day of judgment. In fact, he had stayed living in Prague under the name of Karl Jerhot, and one day he showed up at the local police precinct in the town of Manetin, east of the Czech capital. Turning himself over to the authorities, he is believed to have remarked, "What is to come, let it come."

Tried and convicted of high treason, he was sentenced to death and apparently did not make a request for leniency. He was hanged on 27 April 1947 at Prague's Pankrac Prison. During his trial, the judge asked Curda why he betrayed Josef Gabcik and Jan Kubis. The defendant's response was chilling: "I think you would have done the same for 1 million marks."

ABOVE Some historians believe Curda only gave up Heydrich's assassins because he feared his village would be targeted by the Germans

BELOW Saints Cyril and Methodius Cathedral in Prague bears the scars from a gunfight between cornered Czech resistance fighters and German troops

OPPOSITE The remnants of Heydrich's Mercedes

© Wikipedia Commons

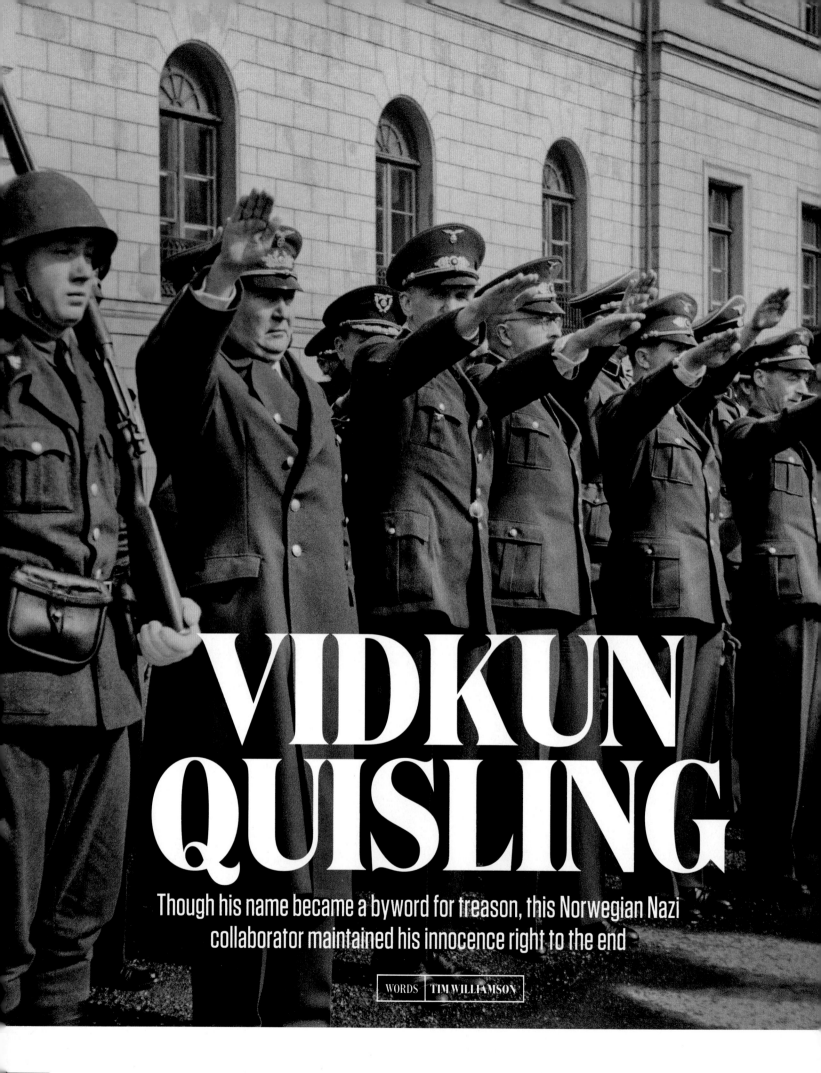

VIDKUN QUISLING

Though his name became a byword for treason, this Norwegian Nazi collaborator maintained his innocence right to the end

WORDS | TIM WILLIAMSON

VIDKUN QUISLING

"Any man or State who marches with Hitler is our foe. This applies not only to organised states but to all representatives of that vile race of Quislings who make themselves the tools and agents of the Nazi regime against their fellow-countrymen…" Winston Churchill's June 1941 address after the German invasion of the Soviet Union is one of the first instances of a new word: Quisling. Soon synonymous with treason, the name in fact belonged to Norwegian fascist leader and Nazi collaborator Vidkun Quisling. Born in 1887, Quisling grew up during a period of intense change in Norway. In 1905, the nation's nearly century-old union with Sweden came to an end after a referendum. It was in that same year that Quisling enrolled in the military academy in Oslo, graduating at the top of his class. After being appointed to the general staff of the Norwegian army, he was later sent to Petrograd to serve as the nation's military attaché. The Russian Revolution had broken out the previous year, and part of Quisling's role was reporting back to his superiors on the developing situation.

In 1922, Quisling joined a League of Nations humanitarian mission to Russia and Ukraine, which was in the middle of a famine that killed an estimated 5 million people. The horrors that Quisling experienced would remain with him, and his reports from his mission detail the desperate and tragic situation.

When he returned to Oslo in the winter of 1929, Quisling was already formulating a strategy to achieve power in the Storting (parliament). In 1930, he published *Russia og Vi* ('Russia and Ourselves'), which espoused racial superiority and fervently attacked Russian Bolshevism. These political views found a home in the Fedrelandslaget ('Fatherland League', or FL) a right-wing, nationalist movement. Quisling was even invited to join the government as defence minister – a fleeting role during which he unleashed the military against socialist strikes and incorporated right-wing paramilitary groups into the Norwegian armed forces in pursuit of rooting out opposition.

Seeking to go further with his racist policies, as well as authoritarian control, Quisling helped form offshoot group Nordisk Folkereisning i Norge ('Folk-Rising of Norway'), a fascist organisation and the precursor to his new political party, Nasjonal Samling, ('National Gathering', NS) in 1933. Heavily influenced by fascism in Germany and Italy, the NS formed its own uniformed paramilitary, named the Hirden, who were deployed ostensibly to protect Quisling at party meetings but also engaged in street brawls with left-leaning groups. Among some NS members, the greeting "heil og sæl" ("Hail and good fortune") was used – bearing close similarity to the Nazi salute – while Quisling himself became referred to as the *Fører* ('leader').

The NS was unsuccessful in the 1933 election despite substantial financial donations from Italian fascist leader Benito Mussolini. Nonetheless, Quisling was gradually able to consolidate support from Norway's various right-wing organisations, including the Norges Nasjonal-Socialistiske Arbeiderparti ('Norway's National Socialist Workers' Party'), a small but zealous imitation of Germany's Nazi Party. Quisling's rhetoric became increasingly anti-Semitic, and NS publications defended the German Nazi Party from criticism. In the 1937 general election, NS received even fewer votes than four years prior. Members left NS in their droves, and Quisling's political ambitions were consigned to relative obscurity – or so it may have seemed.

By the late 1930s, Europe's looming war was being fiercely debated in the Storting, with demands to establish the nation's neutrality. Quisling, meanwhile, was busy securing alliances, and in summer 1939 he travelled to Berlin, meeting several prominent Nazi diplomats and officials, including Alfred Rosenberg, head of Nazi foreign policy and one of the party's most zealous ideologues. During his trip he also secured funding for his party, which he addressed at its annual conference in August 1939:

LEFT Quisling gives a speech during one of his trips to Germany, circa 1941

ABOVE Hitler and other Nazi officials meet with members of the Nasjonal Samlings Ungdomsfylking, Quisling's fascist youth movement

"After years of tireless struggle, with high points and low, we are now… facing the possibility of events that could be decisive for this country too."

The outbreak of war on 3 September created a crisis in Norway, which only grew more desperate after the Soviet invasion of Finland in November. Quisling was convinced that cooperation with Germany was the only way to preserve Norwegian independence. In December, he was invited to the Reich Chancellery for an audience with Hitler. Though he spoke German far less fluently than Russian, Quisling earnestly shared his plans to stage a coup, take control of the government and rearm Norway to protect its neutrality. He also warned of the threat of British intervention in Scandinavia and requested German support. Though Hitler remained sceptical of Quisling's capacity to mount a successful coup, he expressed concern at the prospect of the Allies gaining control of the region and promised substantial funding for NS.

In February 1940, the British Royal Navy raided a German tanker, the Altmark, in order to free a number of Allied prisoners of war. As the Altmark was sailing in Norwegian waters, the British raid violated Norwegian neutrality, prompting outrage in the Storting. Two months later, the British began laying mines in Norwegian waters in an attempt to block off German access to the North Sea and stop its iron imports along the Norwegian coast from Sweden. This made it almost inevitable that Norway would be dragged into the war.

The German invasion of Denmark and Norway, Operation Weserübung, began in the early hours of 9 April. Denmark fell within hours, while German assaults quickly established control of Norway's key ports. The Norwegian Government and royal family evacuated from Oslo, which became occupied by German troops. With Hitler's approval, Quisling made his move to seize power. That evening, he made a radio broadcast to the nation: "Fellow Norwegians, by laying mines in Norwegian territorial waters, England has violated the neutrality of Norway," he declared, accusing the government of abandoning the capital and the people. "Under the circumstances, the Nasjonal Samling has both the right and duty to assume the responsibilities of power." Quisling concluded his address by naming the members of his cabinet, headed by himself. He called for resistance to the German invasion to cease and threatened reprisals for anyone refusing to submit to the new regime. However, King Haakon VII refused to legitimise Quisling as prime minister, meaning his bid for power failed after less than a week.

The battle for Norway continued into the summer, with French and British forces desperately attempting to keep a foothold in the north of the country. Meanwhile, the Germans consolidated their grip on Norway, creating an occupation regime, or Reichskommissariat, led by Josef

> "QUISLING WAS CONVINCED THAT COOPERATION WITH GERMANY WAS THE ONLY WAY TO PRESERVE NORWEGIAN INDEPENDENCE"

Quisling pictured in the Nazi-inspired uniform of the Nasjonal Samling

regime. While the underground Norwegian resistance, the Milorg, waged a campaign of sabotage and intelligence gathering, the tense balance of power between the German Reichskommissariat and Quisling's government began to deteriorate. In August 1943, an Oslo police chief, Gunnar Eilifsen, was executed by the Germans for refusing orders from Terboven. The murder was made lawful by Quisling, and dozens more civilians were subsequently arrested and executed on similarly spurious grounds. The deaths outraged Norwegian society and further demonstrated Nasjonal Samling's subordination to the Germans.

In January 1944, Quisling offered conscript Norwegians to serve in the German army in order to fight on the Eastern Front, but the offer was refused by the Nazis. However, by late 1944 the Red Army was advancing into Norway's northern Finnmark region, and it was joined later by exiled Norwegian forces and resistance fighters. The retreating German forces unleashed a scorched-earth policy, forcing over 70,000 civilians to evacuate south at gunpoint. Meanwhile, the Western Allies had liberated France and were moving east. Despite the seemingly inevitable fall of the Third Reich, Quisling travelled to Berlin in January 1945 to reassure Hitler of his loyalty, perhaps hoping that this could somehow protect him from what was now inevitable.

In May 1945, Quisling surrendered to Milorg forces and was imprisoned at Akershus Fortress in Oslo. At his trial that August, he stood accused of a coup d'etat, murder, treason and embezzlement. Nasjonal Samling had retrospectively been declared an illegal organisation by the Norwegian Government in Exile. Quisling maintained that he had only acted out of patriotism and in the best interests of Norway. His health rapidly worsened as the trial progressed and the evidence was mounted against him. He was barely able to stand when giving one of his final statements to the court: "If my work has really been treasonable, then I would pray to God for Norway's sake that a good many of Norway's sons would also become traitors like me."

Quisling was found guilty on nearly all counts and sentenced to death. At 2 a.m. on 24 October, he was awoken in his cell and ordered to dress. He was then taken out onto the fortress ramparts, where he was blindfolded and his arms were bound behind him before he was shot.

Terboven. All political parties other than Nasjonal Samling were banned, and Quisling was appointed to Terboven's cabinet, helping administrate the occupation.

In February 1942, Quisling was reappointed 'minister president', answerable to Terboven but with control over domestic affairs. One of his first acts was to reinstate a law banning the immigration of Jews into the country. This was followed by the mass arrest and deportation of Jews, many of whom had fled to Norway in order to escape the Third Reich. Approximately 772 Jews were deported from Oslo to Germany before being transferred to Auschwitz, where most were killed. Quisling also created a Norwegian equivalent to the Hitler Youth and made it compulsory for all children between the ages of ten and 18. He attempted to restructure the education system by introducing an oath of loyalty to be made by all teachers to the Nasjonal Samling. When the teachers refused, Quisling had them arrested, and 500 were sent to work camps in the freezing northernmost region of Norway. Many became sick and died in terrible conditions.

The teachers strike was just the first of the many acts of defiance against the occupation and Quisling's

ABOVE A Nasjonal Samling parade in 1942, with Quisling and party officials taking the salute

THE ROYAL LOVERS' CONQUEST

Isabella, Queen of England, and her lover, Roger Mortimer, risked everything to carry out one of the most daring invasions in English history

WORDS | JUNE WOOLERTON

On a quiet September day in 1326 a fleet of boats sailed into the River Orwell. Hundreds of men began to disembark, bringing with them horses, provisions and weapons. At their head was none other than the Queen of England, Isabella of France, and by her side was the man acknowledged to be her lover, Roger Mortimer, who'd fled England years earlier in a daring escape to save his life. Together they came in anger, intent on dismantling the country's government.

Success seemed unlikely. The invading army was small and not even completely sure of where it had actually landed. England's king had the potential to raise a formidable force to oppose it and a huge treasury at his disposal. Mortimer had a price on his head, having been in exile for three years after an earlier revolt against Edward II, while Isabella had committed treason by beginning a relationship with him. An unsteady invasion headed by a traitor queen and an unforgiven rebel sounded like a recipe for disaster. Yet, only weeks later, Isabella and Roger had conquered the country and were on the point of deposing Edward II and taking real power themselves with an ever-growing wave of popular support behind them. One of the reasons this unlikely royal invasion succeeded was their choice of enemy.

When Queen Isabella and Roger Mortimer invaded England on 24 September 1326, they had in their sights the Despensers. The family had risen to prominence in the previous eight years, mostly because of Edward II's devotion to Hugh Despenser the Younger. Edward had a habit of taking favourites, with some rumoured to be his lovers, but Hugh Despenser had more power than any before him. Along with his father, Hugh Despenser the Elder, he quickly accumulated land and money as well as exerting influence over the king's policy and government. The Despensers had become so unpopular that by 1321 they were exiled, and war broke out between the king and the barons who were opposed to his favourites. King Edward was ultimately victorious, winning the decisive Battle of Boroughbridge in 1322, and the Despensers were then restored to the heart of his court. With their connivance, the king inflicted harsh punishments on those who had opposed them, and Edward and his favourites were left unchecked. By the time Isabella arrived with her army, the Despensers were the most hated people in England. As her invading force of just 1,500 men unloaded their weapons and provisions, Isabella sat in a makeshift camp, writing letters to the citizens of London to explain that she had come to free England from the Despensers. There was no threat to the king, her husband, in the letters, only promises to save her country. It was enough to start turning people to her side.

But while Isabella played the part of the desperate queen, risking all to rescue her people from tyranny, she also had very personal reasons for wanting to see the Despensers vanquished. Though she was known to history as the "She-Devil of France", Isabella was actually an unlikely rebel. For most of her marriage she was a loyal consort to her

OPPOSITE Bristol surrenders to Isabella during her invasion of England

ABOVE LEFT The 1308 marriage of Isabella of France and Edward II of England, as depicted in miniature

ABOVE RIGHT Edward II came to the throne as a popular king but squandered the good will of his people through poor judgement

king despite his fickle behaviour. Born a princess of France in 1295 and feted from early on for her beauty, she had married Edward II in 1308 and endured years of humiliation as her husband promoted his then favourite, Piers Gaveston, ahead of her. Isabella saw lands and jewels meant for her given to Gaveston, but she compromised and learned to live alongside Edward and his favourite. She comforted her husband when Gaveston was ultimately executed by unhappy barons. She had stood by her husband as the Despensers rose to power, and when opposition to them first threatened to spill into war, she gave him a face-saving reason to exile them by pleading on her knees for the family to be sent away. She would help engineer an opportunity for Edward to turn on his enemies just months later, but once the Despenser War was won in 1322, she found herself sidelined again. Just months after his victory at Boroughbridge, Edward suffered a humiliating defeat in his Scottish campaign and fled south with Despenser. Isabella was abandoned at Tynemouth in Northumberland and only narrowly escaped. Two of her ladies-in-waiting died and Isabella's loyalty to Edward wavered. In the coming months, she spent little time with him and refused to swear loyalty to the Despensers. When Edward found himself at odds with Isabella's brother, King Charles IV of France in 1324, the Despensers moved against her, taking her lands, her household and her four children.

Isabella joined a growing band of high-born figures vanquished by the Despensers and who were in fear of their safety as the king's favourites did as they pleased. The origins of her alliance with Roger Mortimer remain mysterious, but like Isabella he had also been a loyal servant of Edward II who had turned into an enemy because of the Despensers. Roger, Baron Mortimer, was the son and grandson of men who had supported Edward's father and grandfather in their Welsh campaigns. He had held land in the Welsh Marches on the border with England and had made a wealthy marriage to Joan de Geneville. Mortimer was made lord lieutenant of Ireland in 1316, but as the Despensers accumulated land in Wales, he became increasingly unhappy, and in 1322 he was on the losing side at Boroughbridge. The death sentence that followed his capture was commuted to life in prison. He was taken to the Tower of London from where he escaped on 1 August 1323. It is possible that he and Isabella were already in contact – the Queen of England had been at the Tower in February 1323 while Roger was captive there, and soon afterwards she wrote a letter in support of his wife. Whether Isabella and Mortimer were forming a political or personal partnership at this time remains a mystery. They would next meet again in France, where he fled after his famous escape from the Tower. It was here that they became lovers and plotted their invasion.

Queen Isabella's voyage to France was ostensibly to help her husband. Edward, as well as being king of England, was also Duke of Aquitaine, meaning he owed homage for his French lands to Isabella's brother, Charles IV. Edward didn't want to bend his knee to anyone, but he was also afraid that if he left England his enemies would turn on the Despensers. The royal favourites weren't welcome in France and so Edward stayed put. In 1325, Charles confiscated his lands, and Pope John XXII suggested Isabella travel to France to negotiate with her brother to try and resolve the

> "THOUGH SHE WAS KNOWN TO HISTORY AS 'THE SHE-DEVIL OF FRANCE', ISABELLA WAS ACTUALLY AN UNLIKELY REBEL"

THE ROYAL LOVERS' CONQUEST

situation. She left England meek and mild, promising to bring a resolution to her husband's woes, but as soon as she arrived in Paris, Isabella changed. She negotiated a settlement whereby her eldest son, Prince Edward, would pay homage for the lands on his father's behalf, but she refused to go home and held out until the 13-year-old was sent to her. Her son did his homage in Paris in September 1325, meaning Isabella had no reason to stay in France. Her husband sent the Bishop of Exeter, Walter de Stapledon, to bring her home, but she refused to meet him. When Stapledon tried to publicly shame her into returning by declaring in front of Charles IV's court that she had to go back to Edward, the meek and faithful Isabella disappeared for good. In front of a shocked audience she told the bishop that she would not go, adding that "someone has come between me and my husband." Her brother backed her up, telling the bishop that "the Queen came of her own free will and may freely return if she so wishes. But if she prefers to remain… I refuse to expel her." Isabella began dressing as a widow to show that she considered her husband lost to her – because of Despenser.

Within months Edward was letting everyone know he believed his marriage was in jeopardy because of Mortimer, who had arrived in Paris as 1325 drew to an end. The attraction between Isabella and Mortimer was obvious and their affair became notorious. There are few references to it in the chronicles of the time, but in June 1326 Edward II wrote to Charles IV describing Isabella's behaviour as "improper", adding that she "consorts with our… mortal enemy, Mortimer" and sent a copy for good measure to the pope. Around the same time an argument was recorded between Mortimer and Isabella in which he threatened to kill her after she suggested she should return to Edward. That this dispute took place in the presence of Isabella's son shows the depth of feeling between them. Their relationship was no secret and neither were their plans to invade.

Edward II was so sure of their threat that in January 1326 he gave orders for watches along the south coast of England to seek out letters from plotters. In February, Edward wrote to sheriffs around England warning them to be ready to take arms against Isabella, who he said was being influenced by Mortimer. Meanwhile, the queen and the baron were corresponding with those who opposed the Despensers in England while trying to build up alliances on the continent. In another letter to his son, Edward II told him not to marry without his permission, aware that the heir to the English throne was a useful bargaining tool in Isabella's quest to win backing for her planned attack. Edward seemed to gain the upper hand when the pope ordered Charles IV to cease his support for Isabella and her lover in July 1326, and the chronicler Froissart records that not long afterwards the French king summoned his sister and told her to abandon her plans to invade. Isabella ignored him and journeyed to her own lands in Ponthieu to raise support, and as August approached, she followed Mortimer to Hainault, where she made several deals with its count, William, for support for her invasion plans. One of these involved marrying her son to one of his daughters, and the deal was signed on 27 August. The bride's dowry included money and ships, and within a month Isabella and Mortimer led their army of supporters and mercenaries, as well as the teenage heir to the English throne, onto the boats at Dordrecht and set sail for England on 22 September.

Mortimer's daring escape
HOW ROGER MORTIMER ESCAPED CERTAIN DEATH WITH AN AUDACIOUS FLIGHT FROM THE TOWER

Though known for his love affair with Isabella and the invasion of England, Roger Mortimer had already secured a place in royal history prior to those events. On 1 August 1323, he became one of the few people known to have escaped the Tower of London.

Mortimer had entered the Tower in 1322 after losing at the Battle of Boroughbridge (fought in Yorkshire on 16 March). He was found guilty of treason and sentenced to death, but Edward, in a move he would later regret, commuted this to life imprisonment.

Mortimer wasn't going to let prison stop his work against the Despensers and he corresponded with allies in letters smuggled out of the Tower. Edward intercepted them and, realising the danger, considered having him killed.

Mortimer knew then that he had to flee, and on 1 August 1323, he employed a trick that had worked for another famous escapee, Bishop Ranulf Flambard, by using wine to knock his guards out. While Flambard had got them drunk, Mortimer managed to get some kind of sedative into the wine that was served to them on the feast of St Peter Ad Vincula. Once they were all unconscious, the sub-lieutenant of the Tower – who had mysteriously declined wine all evening – helped make a hole in Mortimer's cell, and along with another prisoner, Mortimer finally escaped through the kitchens, climbing a chimney to get to the roof. The use of rope ladders helped them negotiate the Tower's walls and roofs, and soon after they found themselves in a boat being rowed to Greenwich.

Mortimer was now the most wanted man in the country, but while armed guards searched for him, he headed to Windsor Castle to try and free others locked up after Boroughbridge. After that Mortimer headed to the south coast and the Isle of Wight, and from there made it to relative safety in France. His escape became the stuff of legend and only made Edward and the Despensers hate him all the more.

ABOVE An engraving of Isabella from the 1890 publication *The Queens Of England Volume I* written by Sydney Wilmot

ABOVE Clutching his mother's hand, a young Edward III returns to English shores

1 November
After securing Bristol, Isabella sets up her base at Hereford and sends her forces to capture her husband.

16 November
The fugitive royal and Hugh Despenser the Younger are caught by Henry of Lancaster near Llantrisant.

25 October
Edward II and Hugh Despenser the Younger attempt to sail away, but the weather pushes them back to Wales.

16 October
Since arriving in Gloucester a week before, Edward II remained hidden. When Isabella reaches the city, he flees into Wales on the same day.

26 September
Having marched inland for two days, the invading force takes Cambridge and support for Isabella's cause grows.

24 September
Isabella, Roger and their fleet of ten fishing ships reaches English shores, though the invaders aren't certain of their location.

18–26 October
Held by Hugh Despenser the Elder, Bristol is under siege by invading forces for several days. When Bristol falls to Isabella, Hugh is executed publicly.

2 October
Isabella and her army reaches Oxford, where she is welcomed as a saviour. From here she marches towards London.

2 October
Despite having ordered local sheriffs to organise opposition to the invading forces, Edward II flees London to go to Wales.

7 October
Isabella hears of Edward's run westwards when she reaches Dunstable and promptly pursues.

"EDWARD II ORDERED THE CITY TO BAR ITS GATES TO ISABELLA AND MORTIMER – INSTEAD, THEY WERE WELCOMED WARMLY"

Isabella's first brush with adultery

THE QUEEN OF ENGLAND KNEW FIRSTHAND THE PUNISHMENTS FOR UNFAITHFUL ROYAL WIVES

If anyone understood the dangers facing royal women accused of adultery, it was Isabella of France. As a young queen she had seen her sisters-in-law thrown into jail over claims that they had been acting unfaithfully to her brothers. The consequences for her royal house were nothing short of disastrous.

In 1313, Isabella and Edward had visited her father, Philip IV, in Paris. During the celebrations, Isabella gave purses to her brothers, Charles, Louis and Philip, and their wives. Later the same year she saw the same bags being carried by two Norman knights in London. In 1314, while visiting her father alone, Isabella told him she thought her sisters-in-law might be having affairs with the knights. Philip had them all watched and accused the men, Gautier and Philippe d'Aunay, of adultery with his daughters-in-law. The two men were found guilty, as were Charles' wife, Margaret, and Philip's spouse, Blanche. Louis' wife, Joan, was declared innocent. The knights were executed and Margaret and Blanche were imprisoned.

Within months, Philip IV was dead. Louis became king, carrying on the House of Capet, but he had no consort until Margaret conveniently died in 1315, allowing Louis to remarry. He died in June 1316, and his son, John, born that November, only lived for five days. Louis had had a daughter, Joan, with Margaret, but his brother Philip now contested her legitimacy given her mother's adultery. He became king but died in 1322, leaving only daughters. His brother Charles took the crown as the tradition of male-only succession had taken root when Philip claimed the crown above a woman.

Charles remarried twice after the imprisonment of his first wife, but on his death in 1328 he left no heir, and the French crown passed to the House of Valois. Isabella had not only seen her sisters-in-law suffer as a result of their adultery, but the affairs had led to her royal house losing the crown. There would be more serious consequences, too. Ultimately, the Valois claim to the French crown was challenged by Isabella's son, Edward III, leading to the Hundred Years' War.

THE ROYAL LOVERS' CONQUEST

ABOVE Hugh Despenser the Younger meets his grizzly fate, as depicted in *Froissart's Chronicles*

BELOW Queen Isabella's forces march into Hereford, where she based her operations (another depiction of Despenser's death is shown in the background)

Edward's spies knew where they were planning to land and the king had ordered a fleet of ships to the Orwell, but it never appeared. When the invaders landed they were swift and ruthless in their operation. Isabella was a mastermind at winning public support, and the day after arriving in Orwell she headed, dressed in her widow's clothes, towards the shrine at Bury St Edmunds, reassuring the local population along the way that her troops would not pillage and paying for any damage already done. By the time she reached Cambridge a number of bishops joined her to express their support and hand over much-needed funds.

Edward II, meanwhile, tried to raise troops and asked the people of London to help – he was all but ignored. He gave pardons to murderers if they would fight for him and offered a reward of £1,000 for Mortimer's head. The invaders headed to Oxford and Edward II ordered the city to bar its gates to Isabella and Mortimer – instead, they were welcomed warmly. Isabella was presented with a silver cup, and one of her friendly bishops, Adam Orleton, preached a sermon at St Mary's in the city in her support.

Edward began to flee west while Isabella and Mortimer honed in on London, appealing to its citizens for help. The city turned for the queen in the middle of October, taking the Tower and killing one of Despenser's men. Walter de Stapledon was in London at the time and rode for sanctuary in St Paul's, but he was intercepted and killed, with his head sent to Isabella as a trophy. It reached her in Gloucester after she and Mortimer decided to follow Edward towards Wales. Soon after they claimed their first Despenser after laying siege to Bristol, which was under the command of Hugh the Elder. When the city fell he was tried and executed while his son and Edward II rode hopelessly through Wales trying to find supporters.

As he realised his cause was lost, Edward appealed in vain to Isabella to negotiate a settlement. By the time he was captured, near Llantrisant on 16 November, he had few men to support him, and his wife and her lover were already issuing orders to bring the country back to normality. Edward was sent to Monmouth Castle while Hugh Despenser the Younger was brought before Isabella in Hereford, where he was ultimately condemned on 24 November, dying a grisly death immediately afterwards.

On 26 November, the Great Seal was delivered to Queen Isabella. She and Mortimer were now effectively in charge of England just two months after their invasion began. Edward II remained in custody while a council debated his fate, and in January its decision to depose him was agreed by Parliament. Isabella's son became Edward III, crowned on 1 February 1327, with his mother and her lover in Westminster Abbey to watch. The teenage king might be sitting on the throne, but they controlled it. By the time that news of Edward II's death reached the court on 23 September 1327, Isabella and Mortimer were fully in control and doing little to hide their relationship.

The invasion that began in such inauspicious circumstances had led them to power with little bloodshed. The lovers had freed England from some of its most hated figures, but within three years they were thrown out of power without protest. Accused of seizing powers reserved for a royal, Mortimer was executed by hanging in 1330 on the orders of Edward III. As for Isabella, she would later emerge from house arrest to play a part in royal life once more during her son's reign.

AMERICAN SCOUNDREL: GENERAL JAMES WILKINSON

Confidant to five American presidents, James Wilkinson successfully hid his role as a Spanish secret agent

WORDS | GREG KING

AMERICAN SCOUNDREL: GENERAL JAMES WILKINSON

A decorated soldier who served in the Continental Army during the American Revolution; first Governor of the Louisiana Territory; a confidant of five presidents – and a secret agent for Spain who plotted against his own country. General James Wilkinson was a walking contradiction, a man whose desire for admiration was topped only by a love of money that drove him to betray the country he served.

Born in 1757, Wilkinson came from an impoverished but genteel Maryland family. His future, both monetarily and politically, vastly improved in 1778 when he married Ann Biddle, a member of the important Philadelphia banking family of that name. Imbued with rather contradictory views of entitlement coupled with moral pliability, Wilkinson was a master of intrigue.

Wilkinson began military service on turning 18, participating in the successful Siege of Boston, which drove out the British, before being dispatched to Canada as an aide to Benedict Arnold, another infamous traitor. Wilkinson lied about his military involvement to win a promotion, but his constant intrigues saw him dismissed from the Continental Army in 1778.

After a spotty few years in politics, Wilkinson moved to Kentucky territory, most of which at that time was still part of Virginia. When statehood was denied to Kentucky, Wilkinson came up with a new scheme to enrich himself. In 1788 he travelled to New Orleans, which was then under Spanish control, and met with Governor Esteban Rodríguez Miró, presenting a most intriguing idea. If Spain offered Kentucky territory benevolent treatment as a vassal state, Wilkinson would work to break the lands away from Virginia and ensure that it never sought statehood again. It would become a part of the Spanish Empire. In exchange for this, Spain was to offer the new vassal state of Kentucky exclusive trading rights along the Mississippi River.

Wilkinson did not neglect his own position, of course. He wanted thousands of acres, under Spanish protection, along the Mississippi, and a small fortune in gold coins. Miró was no fool. He recognised that Spain risked war with the new American nation if it pursued such a policy. But he was also cagey enough to realise that Wilkinson might be a useful ally in future Spanish causes. He therefore agreed to enrol Wilkinson as "Agent 13" after the American secretly swore allegiance to the King of Spain. This Wilkinson did, and soon enough he began receiving regular shipments of gold coins hidden in barrels and shipped up the Mississippi River by barge. Thus, Wilkinson became the central figure in what later became known as "the Spanish Conspiracy".

Rumours always surrounded Wilkinson, but although there were suspicions about his potential espionage for Spain, no one in the American Government had any proof. It was a particularly difficult time in the new republic, and maintaining the loyalty of its army was of paramount importance. Concerns were overlooked in favour of necessity. Wilkinson must have been delighted when George Washington promoted him to the rank of brigadier general. He continued as an important army officer under presidents John Adams, Thomas Jefferson and James Madison.

In 1803, Wilkinson took possession of the Louisiana Purchase from the French Government on behalf of the United States and became its first governor in 1805. He used the position to regularly warn Spain of America's plan of westward expansion. This allowed Spain to build defensive lines and reinforce its troops. This delayed the American annexation of Texas.

An inveterate intriguer, Wilkinson also involved himself in the so-called Burr Conspiracy. In 1806, former Vice-President Aaron Burr entered into secret negotiations with the British, suggesting that the southwestern territories would be amenable to forming an independent country favourable to Britain. He also contacted Spanish officials, suggesting a similar scheme. Ever the plotter, Wilkinson joined Burr in promoting the idea in exchange for the promise of considerable riches. When the plot was discovered, Wilkinson doctored letters he had received from Burr and offered them to the American Government. This resulted in Burr being charged with treason. In the end, Burr was acquitted when John Marshall, chief justice of the United States Supreme Court, decided that the evidence presented was insufficient.

Through clever forgery Wilkinson temporarily managed to evade justice, but when James Madison succeeded Jefferson as president he ordered Wilkinson court-martialled. The proceedings were muddled, and the general was eventually exonerated. Aware that new charges could follow, he fled to Mexico City, where he died in 1825 at the age of 68. Definite proof of treacherous activities only emerged decades after his death, leading President Theodore Roosevelt to say, "In all our history, there is no more despicable character."

ABOVE Wilkinson's father once said to him, "My son, if you ever put up with an insult, I will disinherit you"

BELOW This painting depicts the area around Boston during the siege

JULIUS & ETHEL

The only U.S. citizens ever to be executed for espionage, were the Rosenbergs communist spies or victims of a government set-up?

WORDS | BEE GINGER

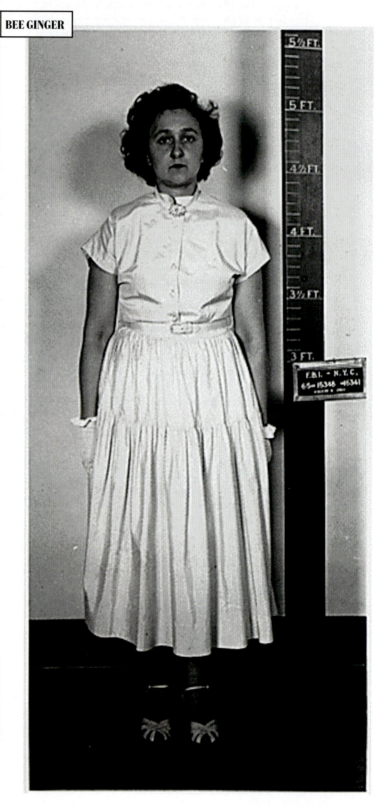

JULIUS & ETHEL

For fans of true crime shows, the shocking story of a Jewish couple put on trial for passing atomic secrets to the Soviet Union sounds like a plot for a binge-worthy box set. But this story is real – and it ends in tragedy.

There was a palpable fear in the 1950s that the USSR would launch an atom bomb at the United States. This fear, fuelled by the U.S. Government, bred hysteria among the American public, a Cold War paranoia that permeated daily life. There were those, however, who supported the endeavours of Stalin's superpower, some of whom even went so far as to join the Young Communist League Party.

In 1936, three years prior to the outbreak of World War II, 21-year-old Ethel Greenglass attended a Communist Party meeting in New York City, where she met a young man by the name of Julius Rosenberg. They married in 1939, and by 1947 they were parents to two sons.

Ethel, who had aspirations to be a singer and actress, was employed at a shipping company in a secretarial role, while Julius, who had a degree in electrical engineering, worked on research into missile controls, radar and electronics for the Army Signal Corps at Fort Monmouth, New Jersey. He was later let go from his position for his involvement with the Communist Party, but not before he allegedly acted as an informant for the Soviet Union by passing on highly sensitive information.

On 17 June 1950, Julius was arrested on suspicion of espionage, and Ethel was brought into custody on 11 August on suspicion of aiding her husband. In court the prosecution painted Ethel as a bad mother for prioritising communism over her children despite a lack of any evidence to suggest that she had actively participated in any criminal behaviour. The case against Ethel hinged on the testimony of a source close to home: her brother, David.

A former sergeant in the U.S. Army, David Greenglass worked in the atomic laboratories of Los Alamos as scientists toiled to create an atomic weapon. Under questioning he confessed in court to having given stolen documents and handwritten notes detailing atomic experimentation and nuclear secrets relating to the Manhattan Project to his brother-in-law, Julius. He also testified against his sister, claiming that Ethel had typed up the information before Julius gave it to the Soviets.

Informants and spies were not uncommon during the Cold War, but the case of the Rosenbergs would go down in U.S. history due to the government's decision to make an example of the couple in the hope of dissuading others. Their determination to secure a conviction is perhaps best illustrated by the fact that a key part of Greenglass' testimony was not shared with the court. Prior to his explosive court testimony, Greenglass had asserted that Ethel was not a part of the actual spy ring. Decades later, in 1996, Greenglass would confess to passing highly sensitive and secret documentation to Harry Gold, a New York chemist and courier for the USSR, and admit to lying under oath. His reason for doing so was to ensure leniency for himself and his own wife and children, simultaneously perjuring himself and condemning Ethel and Julius.

In the end, it was a humble box of Jell-O that ultimately helped to convince the jury of Julius' guilt. Greenglass claimed his brother-in-law had cut a box of it in half, keeping one for himself and giving the second half to Greenglass' wife, Ruth. The court was told that this was to act as a type of covert signal, and when the jury subsequently heard that a man arrived at the Greenglass home, produced half a box of the gelatine desert and stated "Julius sent me", they were on the edge of their seats. Because the two parts of the box fitted together Greenglass said he gave the mystery man sketches pertaining to the design of the atomic bomb. To a jury drawn from a populace terrified by the prospect of communism and a nuclear attack from the Soviets, this was damning.

Ethel and Julius were tried together, and throughout the process they stoically maintained their innocence. When questioned about their involvement with the Communist Party they pleaded the Fifth Amendment on the advice of their legal team. Their silence didn't save them. The jury of 11 men and one woman found them guilty, and they were sensationally sentenced to death under Section 2 of the United States Espionage Act on 19 June 1953 by Judge Irving Kaufman. Nine appeals, tireless attempts to overturn the verdict and several pleas for clemency to two presidents followed, all to no avail.

Three years after the trial's conclusion the couple were executed. Neither uttered a word before they died at Sing Sing Prison in Ossining, New York. Death by "Old Sparky", the original electric chair built for the prison in 1891, was a truly horrendous way to go. Ethel's execution was badly bungled; following three charges she was removed from the chair only for it to be discovered that her heart was still beating, meaning she had to be strapped back in to receive a further two jolts of electricity. Witnesses to the execution reported seeing smoke rising from her head.

To date, Julius and Ethel remain the only American citizens to be put to death for the crime of conspiracy to commit espionage. Their sons, Robert and Michael, have repeatedly called for them to be pardoned. In 2024, they were furnished with a note penned by a former U.S. codebreaker working at the time of their parents' alleged crimes that stated Ethel was aware of what her husband was doing but was prevented from participating in espionage due to ill health. It seems that her only crime was supporting the man she loved.

ABOVE Unable to hide its anti-communist bias, the U.S. media was unsympathetic to the plight of the Rosenbergs

BELOW The trial made news all over the world, inciting outrage and protests, with many asserting both Ethel and Julius' innocence

THE BETRAYALS
OF LÜ BU

Soldier, politician, and traitor, Lü Bu became one of the most powerful figures in China

| WORDS | **CATHERINE CURZON** |

Lü Bu was a general of the ancient Chinese Three Kingdoms era. Massive in stature, a fierce warrior, peerless archer and immensely talented horseman, he was feared and revered in equal measure. His loyalty, however, left much to be desired.

Lü Bu built his reputation under the mentorship of Ding Yuan, the inspector of the Bing Province, who employed him as a personal aide and came to view him as a trusted retainer. When Emperor Ling died in 189 CE, Ding Yuan rallied to the call of General He Jin and led his army to the capital, Luoyang, where they intended to eliminate the powerful eunuch faction, a group of highly influential figures at Ling's court. Instead, He Jin was assassinated before Ding Yuan could reach Luoyang. It was then that warlord Dong Zhuo marched into the city, defeated the eunuchs and took control of the capital. When Ding Yuan arrived he found Dong Zhuo in charge but believed that he too could carve out a role. Dong Zhuo, however, had no such plans.

Though Ding Yuan had taken Lü Bu under his wing and given him a position of trust and influence, Dong Zhuo was sure that the ambitious young man could be tempted into

THE BETRAYALS OF LÜ BU

ABOVE Lü Bu's first betrayal was the murder of his mentor, Ding Yuan

RIGHT Cao Cao had Lü Bu executed in 199 rather than accept an alliance that he couldn't trust

betraying his mentor in return for a position with his own, more powerful, faction. He was right. Lü Bu agreed to betray Ding Yuan and murdered his mentor by decapitating him. He presented the severed head to Dong Zhuo, who now held total power in the capital. In return Dong Zhuo named Lü Bu as his foster son, rewarding him for his loyalty with a series of lucrative promotions.

With the government under his control, Dong Zhuo placed a puppet ruler, Emperor Xian, in power, but this proved a step too far for other local warlords. They formed an association with the aim of deposing Dong Zhuo and his puppet monarch, leading to a series of brutal battles at which Lü Bu proved his ferocity on the battlefield. However, while he was a fierce and terrifying warrior, he was also a difficult man to get along with. As a result of personality clashes with his fellow officer, Hu Zhen, their army fell into disarray and handed the coalition of warlords a significant victory, forcing them into retreat. Warlord Sun Jian made it all the way to the capital, all the time driving Lü Bu further back. So close did they come that Dong Zhuo evacuated Luoyang and moved the capital to Chang'an, leaving his troops to raze Luoyang to the ground. It was to be the last battle for the coalition, which broke up following the capital's move.

Rude and boorish, Dong Zhuo was bitterly aware that he had many enemies on his own side. Constantly alert to the threat of assassination, he kept Lü Bu close by as a bodyguard. However, Lü Bu wasn't immune from his foster father's furious and sometimes violent outbursts, which eventually led him to resent Dong Zhuo, though he kept his simmering feelings a secret from his foster father. He had also embarked on a secret affair with one of Dong Zhuo's maids and feared what

123

LEFT Tired of his foster father Dong Zhuo's violent outbursts, Lü Bu eventually murdered him

BELOW Lü Bu might have won a victory over Cao Cao, but ultimately his success would be fleeting

might happen should this forbidden liaison be discovered by Dong Zhuo.

The answer came soon after the discovery of the relationship. After a particularly violent attack when Dong Zhuo threw an axe at Lü Bu and almost killed him, Lü Bu went to see Wang Yun, an influential politician who had always been an ally, and told him what had happened. Only then did Wang Yun and another official, Shisun Rui, admit that they were plotting a coup against Dong Zhuo and invite Lü Bu to join the conspiracy. At first Lü Bu was horrified at the idea, saying that he could not kill his father, but the two men pointed out that they were father and son in words only, adding that Dong Zhuo seemed to care nothing for the bond when he had almost killed Lü Bu. Lü Bu considered their words and once again decided to place his own interests ahead of loyalty: he would kill Dong Zhuo.

On 22 May 192, Lü Bu greeted Dong Zhuo at the palace gate. Ranked along the wall were a dozen trusted soldiers under the command of the supposedly loyal Captain Li Su. It was Li Su who dealt the first blow, swinging at Dong Zhuo with a ji, a type of polearm, but the weapon glanced off the warlord's armour. When Dong Zhuo appealed to his bodyguard Lü Bu to save him, Lü Bu told him he was merely carrying out an order and dealt the fatal strike. In a final display of disrespect, the corpse of Dong Zhuo was left out in the street with a lit candle wick threaded through its navel. The wick burned on the fat of the dead warlord for days, and people were warned that, should they attempt to intervene, they would be put to death. In the end, three city officials attempted to retrieve the body and were executed alongside all those loyal to Dong Zhuo.

From outside of Chang'an, followers loyal to Dong Zhuo came to the city to seek an amnesty from execution. When Wang Yun refused their request, they instead formed an army and moved to attack the city. Lü Bu challenged their leader, Guo Si, to a duel. Though he drew the first blood, when the armies regrouped, Lü Bu found himself outmatched and had no choice but to flee. The plan to assassinate Dong Zhuo had been a success, but the aftermath was a disaster.

Lü Bu had Dong Zhuo's head displayed on his saddle as a trophy when he and his men rode forth to meet warlord Yuan Shu. As a long-term opponent of Dong Zhuo, Lü Bu made a gift of his former mentor's head to Yuan Shu and expected to be greeted warmly. However, with his reputation for betrayal preceding him, Yuan Shu kept Lü Bu at arm's length. It was still a warmer welcome than the one he received from another warlord, Yuan Shao, who planned an assassination attempt that Lü Bu only just escaped.

Lü Bu travelled on, seizing Puyang and appointing himself governor of Yan Province. Many joined his forces in a battle against the warlord Cao Cao, which is said to have lasted for 100 days. When famine and disease lay waste to the area Cao Cao claimed the victory, forcing Lü Bu to seek shelter with another warlord, Liu Bei. Though Lü Bu was respectful to Liu Bei, the latter understandably didn't trust him, anticipating that betrayal would soon follow. His judgement was proven right when Yuan Shu contacted Lü Bu and thanked him for his loyalty and the part he played in defeating Dong Zhuo. He explained that Liu Bei had started a ruinous war with him and wanted Lü Bu's help in dealing with Liu Bei once and for all. If he would take the job, Yuan Shu promised Lü Bu all the supplies and armaments he could ever need.

Lü Bu accepted the offer and burned the city of Xiapi, taking Liu Bei's family as captives. Outmatched and

> "LÜ BU WAS HORRIFIED, SAYING THAT HE COULD NOT KILL HIS FATHER, BUT THE TWO MEN POINTED OUT THAT THEY WERE FATHER AND SON IN WORDS ONLY, ADDING THAT DONG ZHUO SEEMED TO CARE NOTHING FOR THE BOND"

THE BETRAYALS OF LÜ BU

outnumbered, Liu Bei surrendered to Lü Bu. However, Yuan Shu's promised supplies had not arrived, and Lü Bu believed that he had not upheld his end of the bargain. Instead of taking Liu Bei prisoner, he gave him an official role and declared himself governor of Xu Province.

In 196, Lü Bu survived an attempted coup by his own men, but others were rallying their forces against him. Yuan Shu attempted to broker peace by arranging a marriage between his son and Lü Bu's daughter, an arrangement that Lü Bu initially approved of. However, Lü Bu changed his mind, instead having Yuan Shu's envoy executed when he came to collect the bride. Furious, Yuan Shu formed an alliance with military leaders Han Xian and Yang Feng, but even their combined forces were unable to defeat the seemingly untouchable Lü Bu.

Lü Bu's luck ran out in 198, when Cao Cao laid siege to Xiapi. Seeking assistance, Lü Bu sent word to Yuan Shu, who was in no rush to help. The siege went on for months until, on 7 February 199, Lü Bu accepted that all hope of victory or escape was lost. He told his men to kill him and present his severed head to Cao Cao, and when they refused he surrendered to Cao Cao in person. At first he attempted to negotiate and offered to join forces with his enemy, but Lü Bu's opponents had grown tired of his betrayals. Cao Cao had Lü Bu executed by hanging, ending his chaotic career once and for all.

Brave, ferocious and endlessly ambitious, Lü Bu was an undeniably talented warrior, but with his penchant for cross and double cross, he lacked the strategic skills and long-term vision needed to truly excel as a leader in the nuanced but cut-throat world of ancient China. Making and breaking alliances as it suited his needs in the moment, he was unable to forge the sort of long-term bonds that might have helped him turn his victories into something more permanent. Ultimately, in the final siege, there was nobody for Lü Bu to call upon for aid. He had played the traitor once too often.

BELOW Today, Lü Bu is a familiar character in the world of Chinese literature, theatre and opera

CATCHING AMERICA'S MOST DAMAGING SPY

FBI counterintelligence expert and prolific Soviet spy Robert Hanssen knew the feds were onto him. Why didn't he stop when he had the chance?

WORDS | BEN BIGGS

CATCHING AMERICA'S MOST DAMAGING SPY

LEFT Hanssen was approaching retirement when he was finally identified as the mole behind the revelation of Operation Monopoly

In 1977, shortly after Jimmy Carter had taken up residence in the White House, the embassy of the Soviet Union relocated to a new building, a short drive across Washington, D.C., from Pennsylvania Avenue. The Cold War was still over decade away from fizzling out and relations with the Soviets were tense, while intelligence agents on either side of the Iron Curtain double- and triple-crossed each other in a spiderweb of subterfuge. Seeking an upper hand in the spying game, the FBI ordered that a tunnel be built from a house on the opposite side of the road underneath the new Soviet embassy so that they could eavesdrop on their opposite numbers. But Operation Monopoly was fraught with technical issues, and after construction was completed, the Americans' attempts at espionage inexplicably failed.

At the time, the FBI suspected that a mole had helped the Soviets sabotage their operation, but that wasn't confirmed until 1994 with the arrest of Aldrich Ames. The CIA counterintelligence officer had handed over countless classified documents to the KGB and betrayed the names of numerous agents spying in the USSR, some of whom had subsequently been executed with a bullet to the head. Ames was caught after splashing cash far in excess of his CIA paycheque, as if his colleagues wouldn't notice his fancy tailored suits and new upmarket house. His spying activities across the previous decade could be linked to the loss of many U.S. assets – but not all. Ames was in Rome when Operation Monopoly was active, and besides, he wasn't an FBI employee, so he wouldn't have known about it. Realising that there was another mole in their midst, the CIA and FBI teamed up to root the spy out. It would be some time before they zeroed in on FBI special agent Robert Philip Hanssen.

After years of trawling through leads that went nowhere, busting legitimate spies who weren't the spy they were looking for and hounding one CIA agent until his total innocence became all too apparent, the joint taskforce finally found the smoking gun they were looking for in 2000. It cost them a staggering $7 million – several times what Ames earned from the Soviets (and later Russian) over the course of his espionage career – paid to a turncoat SVR agent who handed over a file of an unnamed U.S. spy for Russia. The file did have an audio cassette tape recording of the spy in conversation with his handler, however. An FBI agent on the mole-hunting team found that this voice was familiar, and when they read the file notes the mole had made, which included a racist General Patton quote, "We want to get the hell over there… then get at those purple-pissing Japs", everything started to click into place: Bob King, an analyst for the FBI, remembered that Hanssen had once used this unusual quote. The team then looked at Hanssen's assignments and movements across his career and, one by one, matched them to the known activities of the mole. Fingerprints in the file were also matched to Hanssen's. Finally, the spy had a name.

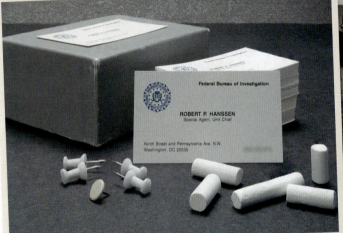

At this point, though Hanssen was still serving as an FBI detailee in the Office of Foreign Missions at the Department of State, he was approaching retirement, so the FBI had to move fast. Special Agent Don Sullivan was assigned to replace Hanssen when he retired, so he was sent to shadow him at the Department of State as the role required. He also had a secret brief to keep an eye on the mole. Sullivan quickly determined that Hanssen had both the means and ample opportunity to access FBI and State Department systems, which were brimming with classified information that Hanssen trawled through at his leisure behind the closed door of his office. So in January 2001, National Security Division Assistant Director Neil Gallagher gave Hanssen a phoney assignment and moved him out of the Office of Foreign Missions into an office in FBI headquarters – a room that was bugged to the rafters with secret cameras and microphones. The FBI soon learned of his next move. On 18 February, he made his final dead drop at a quiet spot in Foxstone Park, Virginia. A surveillance team watched as Hanssen, with black plastic-wrapped documents tucked under one arm, made his way along a tree-lined path to a wooden footbridge where he left the sensitive package. On his way back to his car the trap was sprung: cars rolled up to block Hanssen's exits and agents spilled out to arrest him.

Despite facing the death penalty, Hanssen eventually pleaded guilty to the charges of espionage being levied against him. Over 20 years of experience in the field told him that the crack mole-hunting team had him bang to rights. The task force had indeed amassed an insurmountable arsenal of evidence in their case that, on at least 20 separate occasions over the course of his career,

ABOVE LEFT Hanssen's lawyer, Plato Cacheris, leaves a Virginia courtroom after hearing a judge rule that his client should remain behind bars to await trial, March 2001

ABOVE RIGHT Hanssen initially pleaded not guilty to 21 charges of spying for Russia, 14 of which carried the death penalty

> "HE ADMITTED THAT HE WAS IN IT FOR THE MONEY AND HAD STARTED SPYING FOR THE SOVIETS VERY EARLY ON"

Hanssen had left packages all over Washington for the KGB and its successor, the SVR. He had also supplied his Soviet handlers with around 30 computer discs of data and 6,000 pages of classified information, for which Hanssen was handsomely compensated to the tune of $1.4 million in cash, bank transfers and diamonds. He went by the alias "Ramon Garcia" and used his training as a counterintelligence expert to avoid being detected by the U.S., and to conceal both his real name and employer from the Soviets. For over 20 years, Ramon Garcia was a ghost.

Hanssen never claimed to have political or ideological motivations, as if that would have given him some kind of moral high ground anyway. When he took a plea deal to avoid the death penalty, he admitted to the FBI that he was in it purely for the money and that he had started spying for the Soviets very early on in his career. In 1979, just three years after he had been sworn in as a special agent, he approached the GRU (Soviet intelligence directorate) to offer his services as a spy and he never looked back. But for all his clandestine measures to keep his activities under the radar, Hanssen was prone to silly missteps that he survived only by the skin of his teeth to spy another day. And in hindsight, the U.S. authorities proved every bit as blind as Hanssen was careless.

He once left a pile of cash on a dresser in his house, which was discovered by his sister-in-law, whose husband, Mark Wauk, also worked for the FBI. He knew that Hanssen had talked about retiring in Poland, which was behind the Iron Curtain at the time, and that the FBI suspected one of their own of leaking information to the Soviets. Wauk put two and two together and told his supervisor, who dismissed

CATCHING AMERICA'S MOST DAMAGING SPY

Wauk's suspicions and took no action despite the very suspicious circumstances.

Hanssen came close to being busted after the breakup of the Soviet Union. Fearing he could be outed in the transition from USSR to the newly minted Russian Federation, he ceased contact with his handlers for a year before approaching a GRU agent with an armful of documents at the Russian embassy in Washington. He gave the officer his alias and said he that he worked for the FBI and wanted reestablish himself as a spy for Russia, but instead of bringing Hanssen onboard, the agent drove off and filed a complaint with U.S. State Department, accusing him of being a triple agent. Incredibly, no one followed this up.

Twice he hacked into computers he had no official access to, only to claim on one occasion that he was testing the FBI's security system and on the other that he was trying to connect his computer to a printer that required an administrator password. Both times his superiors believed him and Hanssen got off with a warning.

By the time the investigation had ramped up in early 2001, Hanssen knew that the U.S. authorities were onto him. He rightly suspected that his car had been bugged and in a letter to his Russian handlers he said, "My greatest utility to you has come to an end… I have been promoted to a higher do-nothing Senior Executive job outside of regular access to information. I am being isolated… Something has aroused the sleeping tiger. Perhaps you know better than I."

But the Russians didn't know better. In fact, they only found out who Hanssen was after his arrest was all over the news, with photos of him being frisked by agents accompanied by a damning quote from Hanssen himself: "What took you so long?"

Hanssen was reportedly a good husband and father to three children, with a great career at the FBI. He was also a smart guy; he knew that the FBI was closing in on him yet he went ahead with that final dead drop. Perhaps he was unable to quit the adrenaline rush of spying yet wished something or someone would stop him. Whether they're shoplifters or serial killers, some criminals can't help but commit their particular flavour of crime despite the fleeting and diminishing psychological reward they get from it, despite what they risk if they're caught, and despite the high probability of being caught the next time. In the end, Hanssen's plea deal won him a sentence some might consider worse than death: 15 consecutive life terms without the chance of parole. He died in 2023 after spending 21 years in solitary confinement in the dreaded supermax prison, ADX Florence.

RIGHT Felix Bloch (left), another suspected Russian spy, was being tailed by FBI agents in 1989. Hanssen compromised the investigation so that the FBI could not get enough evidence to charge Bloch

BELOW FBI agents remove boxes of evidence from Hanssen's in Vienna, Virginia, February 2001

HISTORY'S BIGGEST TRAITORS

Future PLC Quay House, The Ambury, Bath, BA1 1UA

Bookazine Editorial
Editor **Charles Ginger**
Senior Art Editor **Stephen Williams**
Head of Art & Design **Greg Whitaker**
Editorial Director **Jon White**
Managing Director **Grainne McKenna**

All About History Editorial
Editor **Jonathan Gordon**
Art Editor **Thomas Parrett**
Editor in Chief **Tim Williamson**
Senior Art Editor **Duncan Crook**

Cover images
Alamy, Getty Images

Photography
All copyrights and trademarks are recognised and respected

Advertising
Media packs are available on request
Commercial Director **Clare Dove**

International
Head of Print Licensing **Rachel Shaw**
licensing@futurenet.com
www.futurecontenthub.com

Circulation
Head of Newstrade **Tim Mathers**

Production
Head of Production **Mark Constance**
Production Project Manager **Matthew Eglinton**
Advertising Production Manager **Joanne Crosby**
Digital Editions Controller **Jason Hudson**
Production Managers **Keely Miller, Nola Cokely,
Vivienne Calvert, Fran Twentyman**

Printed in the UK

Distributed by Marketforce – www.marketforce.co.uk
For enquiries, please email: mfcommunications@futurenet.com

History's Biggest Traitors First Edition (AHB6970)
© 2024 Future Publishing Limited

We are committed to only using magazine paper which is derived from responsibly managed, certified forestry and chlorine-free manufacture. The paper in this bookazine was sourced and produced from sustainable managed forests, conforming to strict environmental and socioeconomic standards.

All contents © 2024 Future Publishing Limited or published under licence. All rights reserved. No part of this magazine may be used, stored, transmitted or reproduced in any way without the prior written permission of the publisher. Future Publishing Limited (company number 2008885) is registered in England and Wales. Registered office: Quay House, The Ambury, Bath BA1 1UA. All information contained in this publication is for information only and is, as far as we are aware, correct at the time of going to press. Future cannot accept any responsibility for errors or inaccuracies in such information. You are advised to contact manufacturers and retailers directly with regard to the price of products/services referred to in this publication. Apps and websites mentioned in this publication are not under our control. We are not responsible for their contents or any other changes or updates to them. This magazine is fully independent and not affiliated in any way with the companies mentioned herein.

Future plc is a public company quoted on the London Stock Exchange (symbol: FUTR)
www.futureplc.com

Chief Executive Officer **Jon Steinberg**
Non-Executive Chairman **Richard Huntingford**
Chief Financial Officer **Sharjeel Suleman**

Tel +44 (0)1225 442 244

Part of the

bookazine series

Widely Recycled